A YEAR WITH NATURE

A PHOTOGRAPHIC GUIDE TO WILDLIFE

To Maria...

best wishes

P Fowl

PAUL FOWLIE

ISBN: 978-1-913450-84-7

A CIP Catalogue Record of this book is available from the British Library

2

Stour Valley Publishing
Haverhill, Suffolk
CB9 9LE

3

4

FOREWORD
OLE MARTIN DAHLE

Since 2006 I have been working as a guide and facilitator in the coastal village of Lauvsnes in North Trøndelag, Norway. In this privileged position I have been fortunate to be able to use my knowledge and passion for wildlife and photography to create some of the most astonishing photographic opportunities for my clients. It must not be underestimated as to the significant effort and skill required to ensure that the photographers under instruction are in the right place, at the right time, and in the right conditions to enable them to encounter and photograph iconic species such as moose, musk ox, sea eagles, Siberian jay and capercaillie in the wild. It is perhaps no surprise then, that I must celebrate The Art of Nature by Paul Fowlie. Paul has taken the time to carefully curate a sumptuous collection of wildlife photography which beautifully presents not only his knowledge of photography, but also reveals some of the very best locations when it comes to capturing on film the stunning species which Britain has to offer. The images Paul has showcased in this book perfectly illustrate the exceptional effort required in order to unveil the habitats of these wild icons of the British countryside. He has dedicated an inordinate amount of his time over many years to help other photographers furnish themselves with the best possible opportunities to create stunning images that would not look out of place on the pages of the National Geographic.

Wildlife photography can be one of the most challenging genres of photography, and in this book, Paul has put in the hours in all weathers, through rain, snow, and hail, to show the reader exactly what is possible should the photographer be willing to expend the required effort, care, and time. It is difficult to precisely convey the levels of dedication, patience, and attention to detail required to obtain images such as these, but Paul has managed to do this so exquisitely.

The reader of this book will receive guidance and practical help from Paul on the kit he chooses and on the methods he employs in order to get sufficiently close to his subjects to showcase them in such eye-popping detail. A Year with Nature can be reached for time and again to serve as inspiration for the budding wildlife photographer's next project, or perhaps simply for a moment's relaxation with the splendour of the natural world – it is sure to be a timeless bookshelf favourite.

Paul has conveniently annotated each image with the precise camera settings used to help the reader achieve the best results with minimal need for any trial and error. Paul's suggestions are certain to be invaluable to those seeking wild adventure yet have such commitments which leave little time to stray too far from home. His guidance will greatly increase the chance of a memorable encounter, reducing the likelihood of the reader making fruitless forays into the wrong habitat at the wrong time of year. There is no doubt that on seeing the results of the fine camerawork and fieldcraft employed in the creation of this book, photographers of all ages and abilities will be inspired to head out in search of a greater intimacy with our wonderful natural world.

INTRODUCTION
CARL MYNOTT

Last weekend I decided not to work at all. Instead, I took a walk in the wild. Whenever I do this I find myself almost instantly rejuvenated. The body and mind's most primal needs seem to be completely fulfilled, enriched by what they find when they are immersed in the British countryside. The absorption of each tiny detail, the richness of colour, the aroma of the air, those delicate sounds, even the buffeting of the wind. Each facet of the outdoors seems to heighten the senses during a walk through the woodland, moorland, mountain and meadow in this beautiful landscape which surrounds us. It's odd then, that it can be said that we spend a great deal of time and money keeping the outside, well... out. We erect fences, seal the windows and doors, put up blinds and isolate ourselves from the sounds of our environment. In our towns and cities, this kind of protection is probably a necessity, due in no small part to the onslaught that civilisation can unleash on our senses. From the acrid stench of diesel fumes to the jarring banging and whirring of industry and commerce, each of these drowning out the more subtle, more beautiful natural sounds, sights and smells that we might otherwise be able to enjoy.

This expulsion of the wild from our home has made bringing something of the outside into our homes somewhat essential. Many of us seek beautiful furniture carved from wood, sprays of flowers to light up the kitchen table, and fabric patterned with floral print, and bright splashes of colour pulled directly from the natural world - daffodil yellow, rose red, forest green, sky blue - which brings me neatly to photography. I absolutely adore taking photographs with my mobile phone when I am out on my walks. The ability to keep these images with me ensures that the wildness of my more natural surroundings can remain close when I am back home, or in the office. From the comfort of my armchair I can lazily flip through those many hundreds of crudely-snatched snapshots, transporting myself in an instant to the precise moment at which that photograph was taken. I am back in the wilds once more, if only in my mind. Is it any wonder then that, when it comes to the artworks in my own home, my walls are filled with stunning photography from unimaginably talented wildlife photographers? Those images, so infinitely more beautiful than my own, offer something so special that it is difficult to adequately describe.

Wildlife photographers, like Paul Fowlie, invest huge swathes of their lives into watching wildlife, learning about the behaviour of their subjects in intricate detail, understanding their movements and habits, and they do it not only for themselves, they do it for us too. The lay chin-deep in the fringes of phragmites beds, or ensconced in an impossibly well-camouflaged hide, their lens perpetually and patiently focused on four square inches of woodland or wild water knowing that one day that moment will present itself.

'Click!'

One-thousandth of a second later the egret is captured. Forever. For us. And we can bring that egret into our homes and wonder at each intricate detail. We can transport ourselves in time and space to that precise moment, frozen in time, when the shutter button clicked.

8

CONTENTS

10

INTRODUCING: PAUL FOWLIE

Paul Fowlie is an international award-winning wildlife photographer. Raised in the North East, Paul now lives and works in the picturesque Yorkshire Dales. He runs wildlife photography workshops for clients where he teaches the skills required in capturing Britain's most elusive and iconic species on camera. Paul is perhaps best known for his intimate close-up images of red squirrels which he takes at his exclusive woodland hide near the beautiful town of Hawes. The inspiration for this book comes from Paul's desire to share his love of wildlife through an exquisite collection of photographs showcasing the magnificent diversity of the British Isles' wildlife.

Paul also teaches clients in Scandinavia, travelling to Sweden for Golden Eagles, Finland for Brown Bears, and Norway for White Tailed Eagles, Arctic Fox and Musk Ox.

GEAR

It is fair to say that wildlife photography can be an expensive affair when it comes to equipment particularly when it is compared to other forms of photography. The need to bring an often distant subject up-close and in sharp focus calls for long lenses and skilful field-craft.

Throughout the book I may refer to lenses and camera bodies that I have used. Similar equipment is available from many other camera brands. The intention here is to share the details of the equipment I have selected to capture the images in the book, rather than to advocate one brand over any other. It can be quite intimidating starting out in photography, and I hope that sharing my choice of kit provides a helpful starting point as you begin your exploration into the incredible world of wildlife photography.

Camera Bodies

A brief note on camera selection:

When photographing wildlife, it's useful to have a camera which can expose at least 7 frames per second (FPS). The Canon 1DX MkII is capable of capturing up to 14 FPS, so it is ideal for use in wildlife photography. The Canon 5D MK 1V is capable of capturing up to 7 FPS, and this 'full-frame' camera also sports a 30 mega pixel sensor making this a good choice as an entry-level, or back up camera. It is well worth finding a trusted photography shop which offers refurbished equipment. These shops can be particularly helpful and can often provide professional grade equipment at a fraction of the manufacturers' list prices.

My camera bodies:

Canon 1DX MkII
Canon 5D MK 1V

Lenses

Choosing a lens for your wildlife photography kit can be quite a daunting prospect due to the cost of some of the longer, 'prime' lenses. When selecting your first long lens, it would be sensible to choose a zoom lens which offers a range of focal lengths (the number shown in millimetres) in a single unit. Something offering a focal length of 100-400mm is ideal.

My lenses:

Canon 500mm f4L IS 11 USM - performs brilliantly in low light and is suitable for photographing wildlife before sunrise and after sunset as may be required when capturing images of Osprey and Black Grouse, for example, where an early start is often required.

Canon 300mm f2.8 L IS 11 USM - not too heavy, and can produce excellent, professional quality images.

Canon 100-400mm f4.5-5.6 L IS 11 USM - an ideal first lens for wildlife photographers, it offers a wide range of focal length making it particularly versatile.

Canon 70-200mm f2.8 L IS 111 USM - a lens I use regularly at my Red Squirrel hides, particularly on my reflection pool. It has the added benefit that it can be used as an outstanding landscape lens.

Canon 24-70mm f2.8 L 11 USM - an ideal lens for wide-angled shots as demonstrated on my picture 'Up the the Sky' on page.... It's also a popular lens for camera trapping and landscape photography.

Accessories

Tripod

A sturdy tripod is a necessity when using a lenses with long focal lengths. Brands include Gitzo (arguably the best, but very expensive), Manfrotto, and 3-legged Thing.

My tripod:

Gitzo Systematic Series 5

Gimbal Head

The gimbal head is the piece of equipment which attaches the camera to the tripod, and importantly it allows the camera angle to be precisely adjusted, fixing it firmly into position. It is an essential piece of equipment and brands such as Wimberley, Gitzo and Really Right Stuff offer excellent professional-standard gimbal heads. Benro produce a good, lower-budget alternative.

My Gimbal Head:

Really Right Stuff

Monopod

A tripod with a gimbal can be extremely heavy, and therefore difficult to carry over long distances. For times when it is necessary to hike a long way to your vantage point, it is worth considering purchasing a monopod. When it comes to selecting a monopod there is a wealth of choice to suit a range of budgets.

My Monopod:

Gitzo

Wildlife Hides

Given that wildlife photographers will often need to wait for very long periods for their subject to emerge and also for the exact conditions for the shot they have in mind, wildlife hides are the perfect addition to the equipment list. They provide added warmth, shelter from wind and rain, and perhaps most important of all, they help reduce the chances of disturbing the very species being photographed. It is important that, wherever possible, the hide can be left in position for a while before it is used. This will give the wildlife in the area time to become accustomed to its presence, reducing disturbance, and greatly increasing your chances of a close encounter.

Whereas some people might collect watches or handbags - it seems that I have built up something of a collection of wildlife hides. I have lost count of the number I have owned over the years - this is due in no small part to the fact that they often get repositioned or destroyed by the elements. So much is this the case that I once recovered a lost hide entangled in hedgerow some three whole fields away from where I had left it!

When it comes to brands, Tragopan produce some of the best hides on the market. The build quality is outstanding, and everything has been designed with the photographer in mind. The Monal V2 (a large large hide for 2 people) is my firm favourite. Wildlife Watching Supplies also offer excellent quality hides and supply lots of other accessories for wildlife observation and photography. Simon King Wildlife Hides are a good choice for occasional use, and there are many hides pitched at those with lower budgets which can be found widely on sites such as eBay and Amazon.

My Hides:

Tragopan Monal v2 (and many others!)

Fieldcraft

Observing from a Distance

Whilst the internet is a valuable resource for learning as much as possible about the species you are hoping to photograph, there is no substitute for heading out to observe them in the wild. I would estimate that I spend around 90% of my time on field-craft, learning about the subject species. If you are unable to use a hide, observing the animal from farther away using binoculars will significantly reduce the chances of disturbing them.

Trail Cameras are an excellent way to monitor wildlife because they can be left in place for days at a time, with no human needing to be in the environment at all during this time. It is possible to buy perfectly decent, low-budget trail cameras.

Landowners' Permission

On discovering a location where you think your target species might be active, it's important that you have the landowner's permission to both access the land, and to leave equipment in place. Once you have established that you are permitted to be on the land, you can carefully position branches and other objects which can be used as perches and platforms which you can bait with food for your target species. It's then possible to return every few days so that you can check your trail camera footage to see if anything has been to visit.

Hide Rental

It's often possible to visit locations which already have hides in place, where you can pay a fee to access and use them. There is a particular advantage in using a facility such as these because they will almost always be in a reliable spot for a given species. Because my hides are strategically positioned, I am able to I offer sessions providing provides access to woodland habitats with one hide featuring a beautiful reflection pool for capturing stunning images of the local wildlife.

www.paulfowliephotography.co.uk

18

JANUARY

RED SQUIRREL

LOCATION:

HAWES, NORTH YORKSHIRE

BLURRED OUT

HOW I TOOK THIS IMAGE

Laying on the ground, I positioned myself at eye level to the Red Squirrel and set the aperture of my lens to f2.8. Focusing close to the squirrel's head, I wanted to try and blur out the squirrel to give the final image the appearance of 'ghosting'.

SS:	1/1600
AV:	F2.8
ISO:	800
FL:	300mm

RED SQUIRRELS IN DECLINE

Red squirrels have been on the decline for many years. This is predominantly due to the introduction of grey squirrels from North America which have unwittingly passed on a deadly 'squirrel pox' virus to the reds. Loss of habitat has also contributed to this decline. Red squirrels tend to favour Scots pine and Norway spruce in which they build nests which are known as 'dreys'. Once red squirrels have endured their first winter, they can live for up to 7 years.

SS: 1/3200
AV: F2.8
ISO: 800
FL: 300mm

WIDE-ANGLED

HOW I TOOK THIS IMAGE

Using a beanbag to support my camera at the edge of a reflection pool, I placed some nuts immediately in front of the lens. Setting focus to approximately 6 inches, I switched off the autofocus to prevent any accidental adjustment. I returned to the hide and using a wireless remote I fired off the shutter when the squirrel approached.

SS:	1/1000
AV:	F11
ISO:	1250
FL:	28mm

HOW I TOOK THIS IMAGE

I attached a piece of kit called a ball-head to a bracket which I had fixed to this tree. This allowed me to position my camera so it was pointing straight up the trunk of the tree, I then added a small metal feeder just above it which I filled with nuts. Using a similar focal distance to the previous image, I once again set focus to manual to avoid any accidental refocusing and activated the shutter using a wireless remote. Getting the shot wasn't quite as straightforward as I had imagined, as the squirrels tended to climb straight up the tree to the feeder. Realising that I needed to persuade the squirrel to approach the feeder from above the lens, I attached some chicken-wire to the setup to ensure that they climbed down the tree directly toward the lens.

SS:	1/400
AV:	F13
ISO:	1250
FL:	24mm

ARM ON CHEST

I placed hazelnuts around fallen tree trunks in a position where the background was free from 'clutter'. Using a large aperture (f2.8) to blue the background, I lay on the ground so I could position the lens at eye-level to the squirrel. This almost always results in a better composition. Red squirrels often jump onto tree trunks then give a little pause and this what gave me the opportunity to capture the striking pose you can see in this image.

SS:	**1/125**
AV:	**F11**
ISO:	**2000**
FL:	**500mm**

Red quirrels love to run along fallen tree trunks and they seem to take the same route when out and about on there travels I often place feed on this tree trunk to get images of them running along it.

SS: 1/2000
AV: F2.8
ISO: 800
FL: 300mm

HOW I TOOK THIS IMAGE

The squirrel in this photograph rewarded my efforts with this lovely pose. The public bridleway sign offered such a great opportunity that it was impossible to pass up. I attached a small container to the back of the sign, filling it with hazelnuts. I positioned the camera ensuring that there was a clutter-free background in the frame whilst still including a good amount of the dry-stone wall.

PUBLIC BRIDLEWAY

SS:	1/160
AV:	F5.6
ISO:	800
FL:	283mm

THE WINTER LARDER

Red squirrels store food such as hazelnuts for the winter. When food is scarce, they can relocate these hidden caches to keep themselves well nourished through the harshest weather.

SS: 1/320
AV: F5.6
ISO: 800
FL: 188mm

TRANQUILITY

SS: 1/200
AV: F2.8
ISO: 1600
FL: 85mm

HOW I TOOK THIS IMAGE

This image was taken at one of my Red squirrel hides. I have created a purpose-built jumping platform for the squirrels which is positioned strategically to capture shots like this. The squirrels climb up a post then have to jump across to another platform in order to get to the food. Once in position, I can focus on a stick which is half way across the gap, and then lock the focus on the camera by switching it from automatic focus to manual. At the precise moment that the squirrel jumps you take a burst of shots with the aim being to capture the squirrel exactly at the focal point of the lens.

SS: 1/800
AV: F4
ISO: 5000
FL: 200mm

NINJA IN THE SNOW

As with the previous image I set this up on my jumping platform but on this occasion, I wanted to get a flatter image, so it looked like he was flying through the sky I pre-focused closer to the landing platform which enabled me to get this flatter image. I set the aperture to f2.8 as I wanted a shallow depth of field in order to just get the face sharp with the snow creating a nice white bokeh background.

SS:	**1/1000**
AV:	**F2.8**
ISO:	**1000**
FL:	**300mm**

FEBRUARY

MOUNTAIN HARE

LOCATION:

FINDHORN VALLEY

LOCATION: FINDHORN VALLEY

From Aviemore drive north on A9 taking the signpost for Findhorn Bridge, if you miss this turn come off at Tomatin which has a charming distillery. Follow the single-track road which stretches for 10 miles until you reach Coignafearn, you will see a small plantation on your left and cars are usually parked here. Walk over the wooden bridge and the Mountain Hares can be found high up in the mountains, when snowing they can be found a lot lower to ground.

34

HOW I TOOK THIS IMAGE

This image means a lot to me as it has won many awards. Heavy snow had fallen in Scotland and throughout England, I set off with my friend with the intention of getting some nice images in the snow only to find our route to Scotland blocked with many road closures,. After 11 hours we arrived in Aviemore to find that it was necessary to dig out a parking space in the hotel car park. In the morning we headed off to the Findhorn Valley at a very cold -10 degrees celsius. The road into the valley was very difficult to drive on but after a struggle we got to the car park and started our hike up the mountain in knee-deep snow. After 3 hours of scouring the mountain side with binoculars I eventually found a mountain hare which was huddled up in a burrow of snow. I had been lying on the freezing cold ground for about 4 hours when he eventually stood up and moved farther up the hill, he paused over another mound of snow which he used as a burrow to shelter from the elements. Standing proud as though on guard with the blue sky background he enabled me to capture an image I never dreamt of. To this day I feel certain that this image was truly meant to be.

SS: 1/3200
AV: F5.0
ISO: 400
FL: 500mm

LICKING HIS LIPS

HIDDEN IN PLAIN SIGHT

In summer the mountain hare's coat is a grey-brown colour which helps them to to maintain camouflage in the heather moorland. Moving into winter they change almost completely to white blending them perfectly with the snow. The mountain hare has an average life span of around four years.

SS:	**1/2000**
AV:	**F5.0**
ISO:	**400**
FL:	**500mm**

Photographing mountain hares requires a slow and discreet approach. It is important to keep your distance and to refrain from making any sudden movements. These are wild animals and you may easily scare them away. There are a few hares in the Findhorn Valley that will sit quite obligingly, and can be quite tame. Mountain hares can spend a good proportion of their day sitting grooming themselves, sleeping, and simply chilling out.

SS: 1/3200
AV: F5.0
ISO: 400
FL: 500mm

38

FEBRUARY

CRESTED TIT

LOCATION:

LOCH GARTEN RSPB

CRESTED TIT

Confined to the Caledonian pine forest, crested tits can be found in and around Aviemore. Wintertime is the best time to see them as they come to ground looking for food. During the summer months they usually stay high up feeding in the pine trees where it is only really possible to hear them. They can be very difficult to see.

SS:	**1/320**
AV:	**F6.3**
ISO:	**1250**
FL:	**700mm**

HOW I TOOK THIS IMAGE

I placed some peanuts in a feeder which I positioned on the ground next to a small tree stump. I then lay on the ground to get an eye level shot with a nice, clear background.

SS: 1/500
AV: F4
ISO: 2000
FL: 500mm

CRESTED TIT IN PINE TREE

Crested tits rarely stray far from Scots Pine and are found exclusively in the Caledonian pine forests in the Scottish Highlands. It has a very distinctive crest and can often be seen clinging to trees looking for food.

SS: 1/500
AV: F4
ISO: 2500
FL: 500mm

CRESTED TIT

Crested Tits are a species which are now protected under Schedule 1 of the Wildlife and Countryside Act 1981. They eat mainly insects and tree seeds and in the early winter store as much food as possible for use when weather conditions deteriorate.

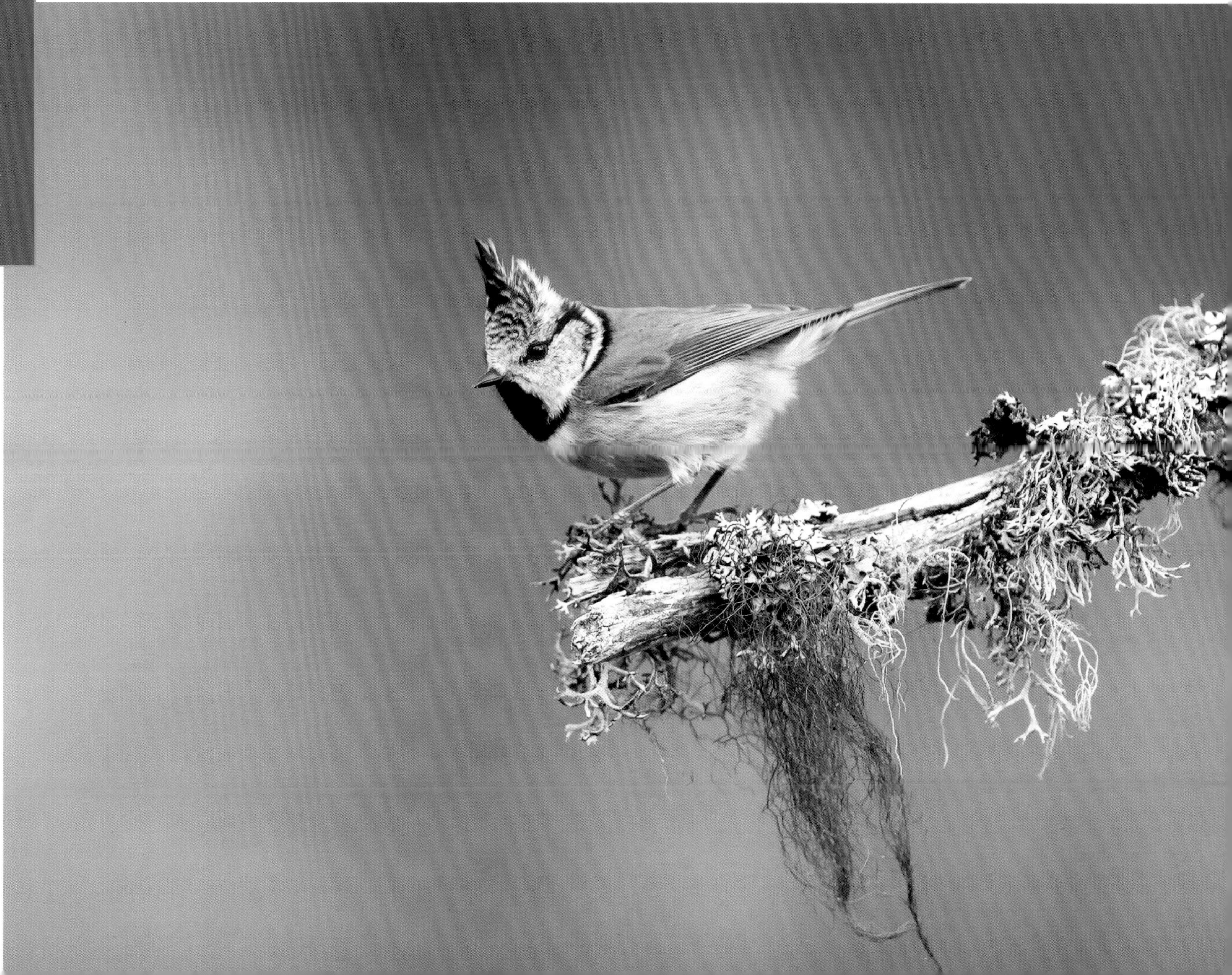

SS:	**1/800**
AV:	**F4**
ISO:	**2000**
FL:	**500mm**

44

FEBRUARY

SNOW BUNTING

LOCATION:

CAIRNGORM MOUNTAIN SKI RESORT

LOCATION: CAIRNGORM MOUNTAIN SKI RESORT

Directions: The Caringorm Mountain Ski Resort is well signpost from the A9 near Aviemore. When entering the ski resort you will find the Snow Buntings on the left-hand side above the car park. Climb up the stone steps and you will find some picnic tables. The Snow Buntings often gather here in large flocks looking for food. Snow Buntings are normally resident to the arctic circle and are a winter visitor to the UK. However there is a small resident population here at the Cairngorm Mountain. The best time to see them is when the snow has arrived as they emerge from high up in the mountains to come and feed among the ski tourists.

BACK OFF

SS: 1/4000
AV: F5.0
ISO: 250
FL: 500mm

SS: 1/2500
AV: F6.3
ISO: 1000
FL: 500mm

50

MARCH

HARE

LOCATION:

FARMLAND THROUGHOUT THE UK

LOCATION: FARMLAND THROUGHOUT THE UK

Unlike rabbits, who live and raise their young in burrows, hares raise their young in a shallow depression in the grass. The young are called leverets and they are able to fend for themselves soon after birth. hares can reach speeds of up to 50mph making them Britain's fastest land mammal. During mating season hares can often be seen boxing and this is where the name 'Mad March Hares' came from. The best time to photograph hares is at dawn and dusk when they are at there most active.

HOW I TOOK THIS IMAGE

I took this picture from a pop-up wildlife hide, this is the best way to get close to hares, this hare bounded straight towards me and was completely unaware of my presence.

SS: 1/6400
AV: F5.6
ISO: 1600
FL: 560mm

WOOLLY HARE

This hare was very obliging, and sat for a while about 7 metres away from me.

SS:	**1/1250**
AV:	**F5.6**
ISO:	**1600**
FL:	**560mm**

SS: 1/2500
AV: F5.6
ISO: 1600
FL: 560mm

HARE PORTRAIT

When going out to photograph hares it is important to practice your field-craft first. Find out where the hares are most active and watch them for a few days. Once you are satisfied that the hares are present every day, approach the landowner (if you have not already done so) to ask permission to place a hide in a suitable position. It is good practise to leave the hide on location for a few days to allow the animals to become accustomed to it. Once it is clear that the hares are behaving normally, you can enter the hide just before first light. This will ensure that they are unaware of your presence. A lot of patience is required with any wildlife photography and if you put in the hours you will be rewarded. This 'Woolly Hare' shot was taken after nearly 2 weeks of sitting in the hide.

SS: 1/125
AV: F5.6
ISO: 2500
FL: 560mm

SS: 1/250
AV: F5.6
ISO: 1250
FL: 700mm

58

MARCH

BADGER

LOCATION:

NATIONWIDE

LOCATION: NATIONWIDE

Setts are usually located in woodland clearings. Badgers are the UK's largest land predator. They are easily recognised with their black and white stripes, but many people never see them as they are mostly nocturnal, only coming out after dark. They live underground in burrows called 'setts' which can have many entrances.   Being an omnivore they eat virtually anything, from small mammals to fruit and bird's eggs. The badger's main source of food is earthworms. Badgers are quite sedentary during winter months, living off their fat reserves and they become more active in March. The female badger (sow) has one litter of cubs per year and they are usually born in February. After a period of around 12 weeks being raised underground, they eventually emerge from the sett during late April/May. May, June and July is a good time to see badgers during daylight hours, usually around an hour before sunset.

SS: 1/320
AV: F4.0
ISO: 1250
FL: 500mm

BADGER CUB SITTING DOWN

Badger cubs usually emerge from their setts between April and May, this cub has been feeding on peanuts I had been placing outside the entrance to the sett.

SS:	**1/320**
AV:	**F4.0**
ISO:	**1250**
FL:	**500mm**

HOW I TOOK THIS IMAGE

In this project, my objective was to capture an image of a badger climbing a tree. Using a food baiting method, I placed some nuts around the bottom of tree and then spread some peanut butter up the trunk. The badger found the nuts very quickly, peeping obligingly around the tree. I fired off the shutter and captured this image. Although he did not follow my script and stand on his hind legs to eat the peanut butter, I was able to obtain beautiful image nonetheless.

SS: 1/250
AV: F7.1
ISO: 1000
FL: 500mm

THE SNARL

SS:	**1/400**
AV:	**F7.1**
ISO:	**1000**
FL:	**500mm**

BADGER

Badgers are very active during the night. They busy themselves repairing their sett, and they spend a great deal of time eating. On a typical day a single badger will eat hundreds of earthworms.

SS: 1/400
AV: F4.0
ISO: 1250
FL: 500mm

BADGER

SS: 1/400
AV: F4.0
ISO: 1250
FL: 500mm

BADGERS IN BARN

In this project I spent 5 months encouraging badgers to feed in the doorway of a Yorkshire Dales stone barn. They are now sufficiently predictable and I am able to run workshops in the evenings to teach clients how to photograph these beautiful mammals.

SS: 1/160
AV: F4.0
ISO: 500
FL: 300mm

BADGERS IN BARN

I placed some peanuts at the front of the barn door to attract this badger who actually has a set under the barn. I then used a continuous light to dimly illuminate the barn door so I could get a focus with my camera. I then set up a flash at 1/128 power to gently light the badger when he came out to feed.

SS:	1/160
AV:	F4.0
ISO:	500
FL:	300mm

SS: 1/160
AV: F4.0
ISO: 500
FL: 300mm

Tricks of the Trade - How I Baited the Badger

I purchased an automatic domestic pet feeder and attached it to a wall in the barn. It was set to release peanuts from the machine twice a day to the sound of a whistle. After a while the badgers became accustomed to the sound and realised that there would be feed on the ground. This also saves having to be on-location every day because a freshly-filled feeder lasts about five days. In addition, I attached a battery-operated security light to a post outside the barn. This was triggered so that it would switch on in the presence of any movement within the barn with the added advantage that the badgers would become comfortable with the lighting. On the days where I wanted to photograph the badgers, I would lay down extra feed in the doorway of the barn which would greatly increase the likelihood that the animals would pause in exactly the spot I had planned to capture them in the frame.

APRIL

BLACK GROUSE

LOCATION:

MOORLANDS THROUGHOUT THE UK

LOCATION: MOORLANDS THROUGHOUT THE UK

The black grouse is a large game bird which is found on moorlands. They are a shy bird which is far less likely to be seen than it's far more widespread relative, the red grouse. Unlike the red grouse, black grouse is a protected species. During March and April, the black grouse congregate in territories known as leks. This is where the cock birds gather to ritualistically fight each other with the sole aim of attracting a mate. During this courtship ritual they display their tail feathers, calling out while jumping in the air. This is called a 'flutter-jump'.

Deliberately selecting a slower shutter speed, I was able to produce an image which conveyed the motion of the black grouse's 'flitter-jump' whilst keeping the rest of the bird in focus.

SS: 1/640
AV: F5.0
ISO: 2500
FL: 263mm

STAND OFF

Two black grouse square up to each other at the lek. More often than not, this behaviour is a flambuoyance resulting in the weaker, less confident birds backing off. Occasionally though, fights break out and can become quite violent affairs.

By far and away the best way to get close enough to photograph the lek is to use a hide. In the same way as I did with the hares, I placed the hide very close to the lekking ground, leaving it in place for a few days until they grew accustomed to its presence. Around an hour before first light, I enter the hide so that the birds are totally unaware of my presence when they eventually emerge at the lek.

SS:	1/1600
AV:	F4.0
ISO:	3200
FL:	500mm

During the courtship ritual black grouse display their tail feathers, calling out while jumping in the air in a 'flutter jump'.

SS:	1/2500
AV:	F5.6
ISO:	1000
FL:	700mm

THIS WAY TO THE LEK

SS: 1/400
AV: F5.6
ISO: 5000
FL: 400mm

Two male black grouse square upto each other at the lek. Just one example of this incredible courtship ritual.

SS:	1/6400
AV:	F4.0
ISO:	2000
FL:	500mm

COO

A wide range of behaviours are exhibited during the lek. The 'coo' involves the male black grouse leaning forward and strutting about whilst making an incredible cooing sound. It is possible to see the males' necks inflating in order to create the sound - a truly fascinating experience to witness.

SS: 1/4000
AV: F4.0
ISO: 640
FL: 500mm

This is what it's all about - the squaring up to each other at the lek has the sole purpose of grabbing the attention of the gorgeous female black grouse

SS: 1/320
AV: F5.6
ISO: 4000
FL: 350mm

SS: 1/2500
AV: F2.8
ISO: 1000
FL: 300mm

SS: 1/250
AV: F2.8
ISO: 2000
FL: 300mm

84

APRIL

DIPPER

LOCATION:

WEST BURTON FALLS, NORTH YORKSHIRE

LOCATION:NORTH YORKSHIRE

Location: West Burton Falls, North Yorkshire, Cotter Force, Hawes, DL8 3LR

West Burton Falls are also known as 'Cauldron Falls' and they are in the pretty village of West Burton in the Yorkshire Dales. Cauldron Falls is a waterfall on Walden Beck in the village of West Burton. There is limited parking and the falls are just a few seconds walk from the car. Dippers often nest under the waterfall and with patience you will be rewarded with good sightings. The falls are a very popular tourist spot, so it is advised to arrive very early. A word of caution, too - the rocks at this location can be extremely slippery after rainfall.

Location: Cotter Force

A small waterfall on Cotterdale Beck. There is a wheelchair accessible walk to the waterfall that takes less than 10 minutes. Watch for Dippers flying down along the bank on your walk to the waterfall. This is a good place to see them but you will not get as close to photograph them as you will at West Burton. Nonetheless, the visit will be rewarding.

DIPPER

Dippers are a medium-sized bird, most often seen on fast flowing rivers or streams where they bob up and down on the rocks. They feed on underwater invertebrates and can often be seen swimming with their head under the water as they search for food. These birds are unusual in that they have a third eyelid which enables them to see under water.

SS: 1/1600
AV: F5.6
ISO: 640
FL: 700mm

DIPPER WITH CHICK

Clutches of usually four to five eggs are laid between March and May. The young leave their nest about three weeks after hatching and are fed by the adult birds for a further week once they have fledged.

SS:	1/1600
AV:	F4.5
ISO:	2000
FL:	420mm

SS: 1/160
AV: F5.6
ISO: 640
FL: 560mm

DIPPER

I had been watching this dipper feeding her young for a couple of hours on a red-hot day. Every so often she hid in the shade of some trees which were hanging down over the beck. I positioned myself down on the rocks and, using some camouflage, lay in wait until she arrived. The sun peeping through the trees produced a lovely backdrop for this obliging individual.

SS:	1/800
AV:	F5.6
ISO:	2500
FL:	560mm

This dipper had managed to catch a small fish for her brood. I was fortunate to witness this dipper strike the fish on the rocks to kill it before feeding it to her young.

SS: 1/250
AV: F5.6
ISO: 640
FL: 1250mm

APRIL

GREAT SPOTTED WOODPECKER

LOCATION:

LOW BARNS NATURE RESERVE, BISHOP AUCKLAND

LOCATION:BISHOPAUCKLAND

Location: Low Barns Nature Reserve, Bishop Auckland
DL14 0AG

With patience at this location it is practically guaranteed to get a good, close-up sighting of the stunning great spotted woodpecker from the woodland hide.

Widespread in woodland habitat, the great spotted woodpecker has a shock-absorbing skull which enables it to hammer on trees to reveal its food. It also uses this hammering action to excavate material from dead and dying trees to make its nest. Eggs are usually laid in March to April. The male and female birds are similar, but the male has a red patch on the back of its head which is not present in the female.

This is one of my favourite Woodpecker images. I was actually in position in a hide waiting for little owls to settle on this post which I had filled with meal-worms. It was a very cold morning with the temperature hovering around -8 degrees Celsius and there was a heavy frost. The post is richly adorned with lichen and there is some old barbed wire lower down which contributes some additional interest to the images. Despite the little owls not making an appearance, the woodpecker certainly made up for it.

SS: 1/1000
AV: F4.5
ISO: 1000
FL: 265mm

SOAKED

HOW I TOOK THIS IMAGE

On this occasion I had positioned myself laying low to the ground with camouflage material covering me (these-days it is possible to purchase low-level hides which are excellent, and far more comfortable). I baited a tree stump with 'flutter butter' which attracted a very wet woodpecker who provided me the opportunity to capture this very nice image. It is often the case that getting the shot you want means you have to get very cold, and very wet!

SS:	**1/120**
AV:	**F11**
ISO:	**2000**
FL:	**500mm**

TEA TIME

Both the male and female great spotted woodpecker take turns in feeding their young. They feed on a diet of insects, tree seeds, nuts and even young birds and eggs from time to time. They have been known to hammer through bird boxes to get at young chicks inside.

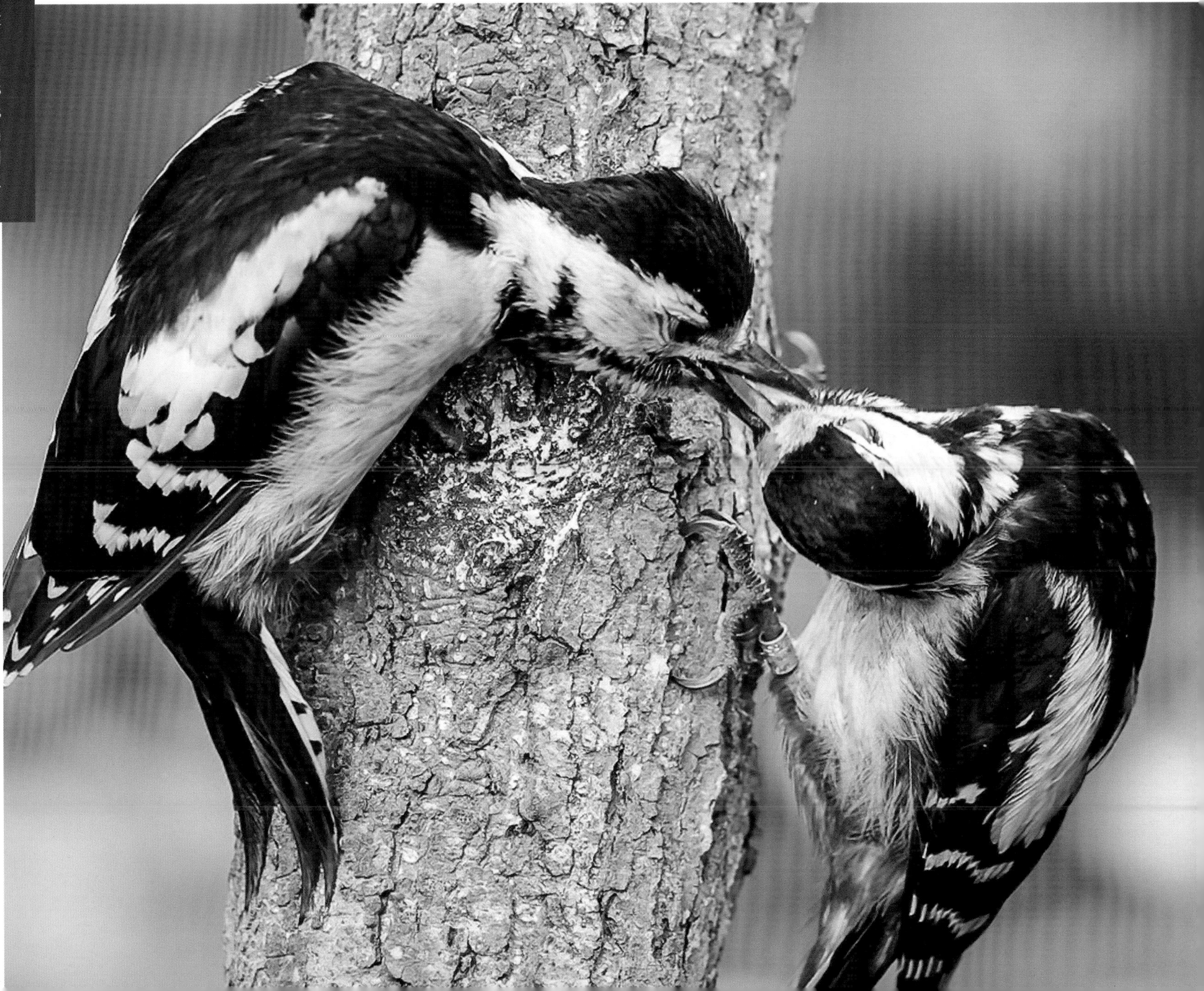

SS:	**1/200**
AV:	**F4**
ISO:	**640**
FL:	**500mm**

BLINDING LIGHT

This image was taken very early in the morning, shortly after sunrise. There was some gorgeous light falling on the post which I had previously baited with meal-worms. In addition to using their beaks to find food, they also hammer on trees to also proclaim ownership of their territory.

SS: 1/8000
AV: F4.0
ISO: 1200
FL: 400mm

This was taken at the blue hour. The golden hour occurs just after sunrise and before sunset. The blue hour arrives shortly before sunrise and after sunset which rewards the photographer with a lovely blue glow.

SS: 1/250
AV: F2.8
ISO: 2500
FL: 300mm

GREAT SPOTTED WOODPECKER

SS:	1/3200
AV:	F5.6
ISO:	1000
FL:	560mm

APRIL

GREEN WOODPECKER

LOCATION:

WIDESPREAD THROUGHOUT THE UK

LOCATION: NORTH YORKSHIRE

Location: Osmotherley, North Yorkshire. Also widespread throughout the UK.

Watch out for them on the heather moorlands at Osmotherley. The green woodpecker is the largest of our three woodpeckers. They nest in holes in trees like the great spotted woodpecker and is most often seen on the ground searching for ants - their main source of food.

In much the same way as with the great spotted woodpecker, both male and female green woodpeckers are very similar in appearance. The male, however, has a red stripe or 'moustache'.

SS: 1/1000
AV: F5.6
ISO: 800
FL: 700mm

GREEN WOODPECKER

The next few images show green woodpeckers on the lookout for ants which represent a significant part of their diet.

SS:	**1/1250**
AV:	**F5.6**
ISO:	**800**
FL:	**700mm**

GREEN WOODPECKER

Green Woodpecker on the search for ants. They just cannot get enough of them! Green woodpeckers like the Great Spotted Woodpecker excavate holes in trees, but they have much softer beaks so usually prefer softer wood in which to make their nests.

SS: 1/2500
AV: F5.6
ISO: 400
FL: 560mm

MORNING DEW

SS:	1/320
AV:	F5.6
ISO:	2500
FL:	560mm

GREEN WOODPECKER

Green woodpeckers have a very distinctive call which sounds like a loud, fluting laugh. This is known as a 'yaffle'.

SS: 1/4000
AV: F4
ISO: 400
FL: 400mm

MALE WITH JUVENILE

Green Woodpeckers usually pair for life but outside of courtship period they tend to spend their time year by themselves. They have one brood per year, each with as many as seven eggs which are usually laid in May.

SS: 1/640
AV: F8.0
ISO: 1250
FL: 500mm

JUVENILE GREEN WOODPECKER

When the juveniles fledge, the parents usually take responsibility for half the brood each to nurture them to independence.

SS: 1/640
AV: F8.0
ISO: 1250
FL: 500mm

112

MAY

WHITE-TAILED EAGLE

LOCATION:

ISLE OF MULL

LOCATION: ISLE OF MULL

The Isle Of Mull is the second largest island of the Inner Hebrides. To get to Mull you will need to board a ferry. The most popular crossing being Oban to Craignure with Caledonian Macbrayne (CalMac). Mull has an abundance of wildlife and in the following pages I've just covered a small amount of what you might expect to see. Whilst you are on Mull it is well worth taking some time to visit the small island of Iona. It is very easy to get to Iona from Fionnphort on a passenger ferry which takes just 10 minutes. It is on Iona where you may be fortunate enough to catch a glimpse of the elusive Corncrake.

WHITE-TAILED EAGLE

To get the best sighting of the white-tailed eagle close-up, book yourself on a boat trip with Mull Charters. The eagles often follow the boat and dive into the sea for the fish which the tour operators throw overboard. It is unlikely that you will ever get closer to a such a magnificent eagle as they dive within metres of the boat - a truly unforgettable experience.

For those who aren't so keen on boats, it is possible to contact Mull Eagle Watch to view the birds at Craignure Golf Course or at their other hide at Glen Seilisdeir.
Tel: 01680 812556
Web: www.mulleaglewatch.com

SS: 1/8000
AV: F5.6
ISO: 1000
FL: 321mm

SS: 1/3200
AV: F7.1
ISO: 1250
FL: 278mm

WHITE-TAILED EAGLE CATCHING A FISH

The white-tailed eagle is often referred to as the sea eagle. It's the largest bird of prey in the UK with a wingspan of up to 2.5 metres. They feed on fish but will also take birds, rabbits, and hares.

SS:	1/6400
AV:	F5.0
ISO:	1000
FL:	176mm

There is a small population of white-tailed eagles in Britain which are found on the highlands and islands of Scotland. In Britain they are non-migratory, spending their winter nest-building in trees. The first eggs are typically laid around March and on a good year they can raise three young. If surviving the first year they can live for over 20 years but according to studies, up to 70% of young sea eagles don't survive their first year.

SS: 1/640
AV: F6.3
ISO: 1250
FL: 360mm

WHITE-TAILED EAGLE

I wanted to capture the full power of the sea eagle as they come in to grab a fish so I selected a 300mm prime lens to get as close in as possible. The next picture shows the bird grabbing the fish.

SS:	1/2000
AV:	F6.3
ISO:	1250
FL:	300mm

SS: 1/2000
AV: F6.3
ISO: 1250
FL: 300mm

MAY
OTTER

LOCATION:

ISLE OF MULL

LOCATION: ISLE OF MULL

Prime locations for otter-watching: Loch Na Keal, Loch Scridain, Loch Beg, Craignure Ferry, Croggan.

The Isle Of Mull is one of the best places in the UK to see otters but with over 300 miles of coastline it's not always easy to find them. There is never a good or bad time to spot them but I have found that I have enjoyed most success at dusk and dawn. Trying to spot one onshore is near impossible as they camouflage in the seaweed. Using your binoculars to scout the sea around fifteen metres from the shore will help you locate an otter which you can then follow as it swims to shore. They can hold their breathe under water for five minutes but usually just dive down for thirty seconds or so as they search for food. Otters have an excellent sense of smell so you will need to be sure to move into the wind, blowing your scent away from the otter. Once they come ashore they can often spend quite some time simply grooming and resting.

HOW I TOOK THIS IMAGE

This otter had been moving in and out of the water for more than an hour whilst it was feeding. I managed to creep quite close to the animal, laying as still as possible on the wet kelp. He surfaced from the water with this pipefish wrapped around his head practically right in front of me allowing me to capture this image.

SS: 1/400
AV: F5.6
ISO: 1250
FL: 400mm

SS: 1/800
AV: F6.3
ISO: 1250
FL: 526mm

Mother and cub having a sleep after a hard morning's fishing.

SS: 1/640
AV: F6.3
ISO: 1250
FL: 381mm

DOG OTTER

I had followed this dog otter swimming about in a loch for over an hour before he came out for a rest. It is amazing how quickly these animals can dry themselves in the seaweed.

SS:	1/1000
AV:	F6.3
ISO:	1250
FL:	560mm

Here is a dog otter enjoying a little snooze. I followed this male as he dipped in and out of the water foraging for shellfish.

SS: 1/1000
AV: F6.3
ISO: 1250
FL: 274mm

SS: 1/5000
AV: F6.3
ISO: 1250
FL: 560mm

As you can see, otters conceal themselves extremely well in the seaweed. Their natural colouring makes them particularly difficult to pick out in this bladder wrack.

SS: 1/800
AV: F6.3
ISO: 1250
FL: 526mm

OTTER ON SEAWEED

SS: 1/1250
AV: F5.0
ISO: 400
FL: 420mm

This was quite a comical moment as I spotted this otter hitching a lift on the back of a boat. Moments before this photograph was taken he was just basking in glorious sunshine.

SS: 1/8000
AV: F4.0
ISO: 400
FL: 500mm

ON THE PIER

Otters regularly climb onto this old pier at Croggan overlooking Loch Spelve to rest and doze off. As you drive toward Croggan after leaving the main road, it's possible to see peacocks in the first field you pass. This route is mostly single track road with very few passing places. Watch out for buzzard, common sandpiper, ringed plover, grey heron, oystercatcher, and wheatear, as well as many other species as you make your way to the loch.

SS: 1/1250
AV: F4.0
ISO: 1250
FL: 500mm

136

MAY

STONECHAT

LOCATION:

GRASSPOINT

LOCATION: GRASSPOINT

Directions: Leave Craignure south-west on A849 and after approximately five miles 8km you will see a signpost for Grasspoint on the left. I just adore stonechats and here is a great place to spend a few hours photographing them. May is a good time to observe them as they are more likely to have young to feed. After turning left toward Grasspoint you will find yourself on a single-track road for a few miles before you reach a stone humpback bridge. Just a half a mile or so further on you can park on the right hand side. It's a popular spot for approaching a small hill where it is possible to look out for hen harrier as they fly over. Buzzards and cuckoos can also be seen here in Summer, and there is always the chance of a flypast from a white-tailed tailed eagle.

JUVENILE STONECHAT ON GORSE TREE

SS: 1/1000
AV: F5.6
ISO: 200
FL: 700mm

Follow the road watching out for buzzards on the telegraph poles. The route winds its way up a very steep hill and once down the other side you will usually be greeted by a herd of Highland cattle, also in the field to the left you can often red deer, especially later in the evening.

SS: 1/4000
AV: F4.0
ISO: 1000
FL: 500mm

A SOAKED JUVENILE STONECHAT

As you approach Grasspoint there is a small car park on right which is large enough for about half a dozen cars, just before you get to the car park is the best place to spot stonechat as they will be flitting amongst the grasses. It is a great spot to pull over onto the verge to wait for them to fly near.

SS:	1/500
AV:	F6.3
ISO:	1000
FL:	700mm

SS: 1/1250
AV: 6.3
ISO: 640
FL: 700mm

MALE STONECHAT

Take a stroll from the car park until you come to Grasspoint, only about a ten minute walk, from here you can often see Otters, porpoises and dolphins.

SS:	1/3200
AV:	F5.6
ISO:	800
FL:	700mm

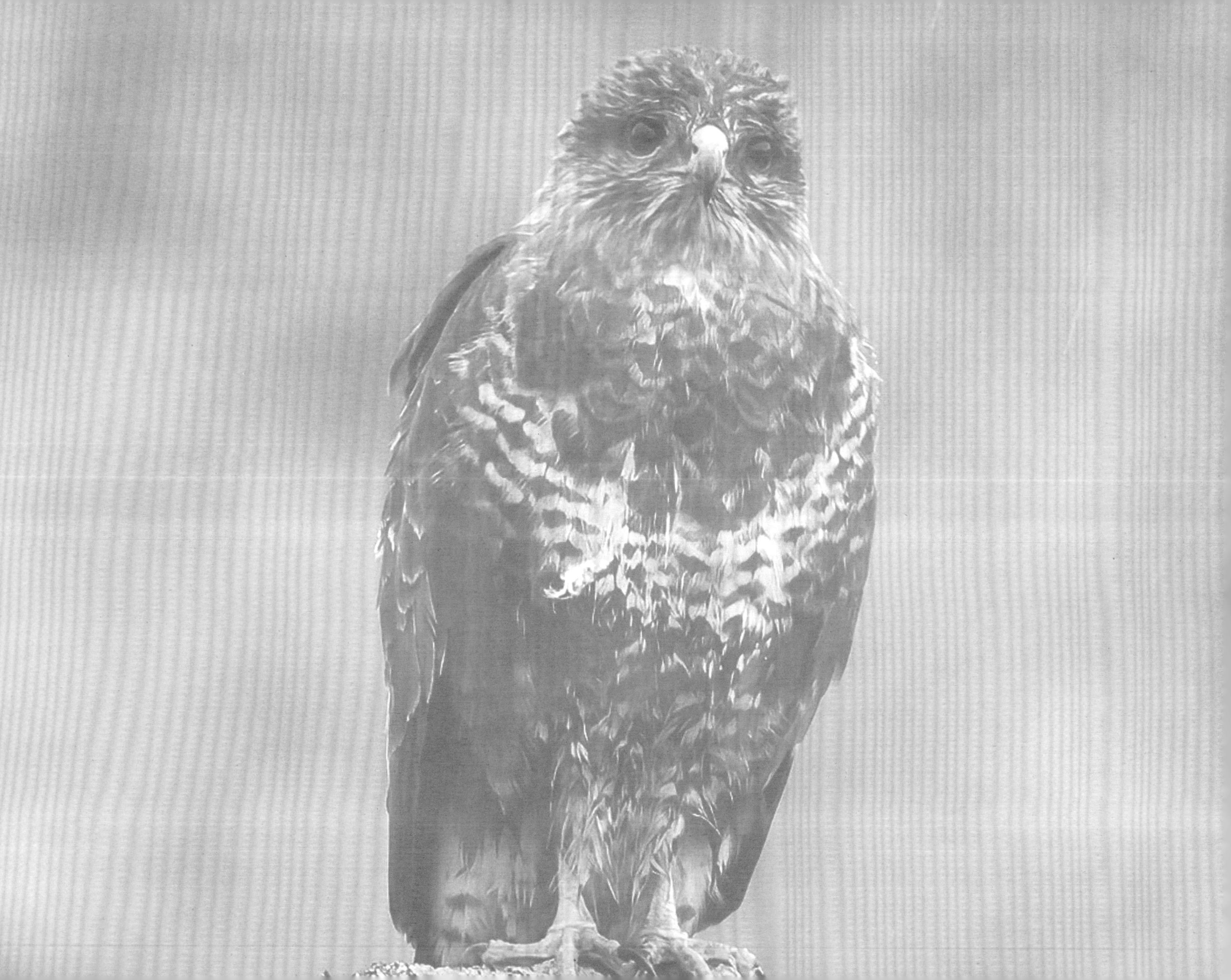

MAY

BUZZARD

LOCATION:

GRASSPOINT

WET BUZZARD

Grasspoint is an excellent place to spot buzzards, but they are widespread across the island. Watch out for buzzards on the telegraph poles and soaring over woodland. Buzzards are now the most common bird of prey in the UK. Their population has quadrupled since 1970. They eat just about anything, favouring voles, rabbits and carrion.

SS:	1/320
AV:	F5.6
ISO:	1250
FL:	700mm

BUZZARD

I captured this shot of a buzzard stretching its wings whilst I sitting in a hide in a field. I had noticed that they were regularly landing in the field feeding so I set up near the carcass of a pheasant and waited. Six hours later, I was rewarded with the appearance of this fine bird.

SS: 1/3200
AV: F4.0
ISO: 800
FL: 300mm

BUZZARD SITTING ON POST

SS: 1/400
AV: F6.3
ISO: 400
FL: 700mm

BUZZARD EATING A FROG

I spotted this Buzzard at Grasspoint at the same location over the few days. After a little time spent observing the bird I discovered that it was feeding on frogs which were in abundance over around an acre of grassland.

SS:	**1/400**
AV:	**F5.6**
ISO:	**400**
FL:	**700mm**

MAY
CUCKOO

LOCATION:

GRASSPOINT

CUCKOO

Cuckoos are found on woodland edges and grassland throughout the UK. The cuckoo is far more often heard than seen with it's unmistakable call being heard in the UK from April until late June/early July when they make their journey back to Africa. At first glance the cuckoo can look like a pigeon or dove, until you are able to get a clear view of their distinctive, barred chest-plumage. This plumage is very similar to that of the sparrowhawk. Cuckoos lay their eggs in other birds' nests, and they seem to favour the meadow pipit and reed warbler. They lay a single egg in the unsuspecting host's nest and once hatched the chick will push the other eggs and even the host's chicks out of the nest. It's quite amazing to see the likes of a small reed warbler feeding a huge cuckoo chick. Cuckoos feed on a wide range of invertebrates and they certainly seem to enjoy feeding on hairy caterpillars. If you happen to find such a caterpillar whilst you are in an area where you have seen or heard a cuckoo, pop it on an exposed post or stump and there's a particularly good chance the cuckoo will take advantage of the tasty snack.

SS:	1/8000
AV:	F5.6
ISO:	1250
FL:	500mm

FEMALE CUCKOO

This photograph was taken in the Yorkshire Dales. The cuckoo was baited by putting mealworms in a small container that was fastened to a nearby post.

SS: 1/800
AV: F5.6
ISO: 1250
FL: 560mm

FEMALE CUCKOO

SS: 1/1000
AV: F5.6
ISO: 1250
FL: 560mm

SS: 1/800
AV: F4.0
ISO: 2500
FL: 400mm

REED WARBLER AND CUCKOO

This photo shows a reed warbler checking on 'her' cuckoo chick. Both the male and female reed warbler came in at regular, seven-minute intervals during the two hours I spent watching them.

SS:	**1/250**
AV:	**F10**
ISO:	**400**
FL:	**255mm**

SS: 1/250
AV: F10
ISO: 400
FL: 255mm

TASTY FLY

SS:	1/250
AV:	F10
ISO:	400
FL:	255mm

CUCKOO IN FLIGHT

It could be argued that I used too high an ISO setting in capturing this shot. I wanted to grab as much light as possible so I could use a fast shutter speed - the objective being to 'freeze' the bird in flight. Nevertheless, it worked out well in the end. This image shows the cuckoo just as it was flying toward a perch which I baited.

SS: 1/8000
AV: F6.3
ISO: 2000
FL: 500mm

162

MAY

COMMON SANDPIPER

LOCATION:

THE LOCHS AND LOCHANS OF MULL —————

COMMON SANDPIPER

The Common Sandpiper is a small wading bird being only 19-21cm in length. It breeds along fast flowing rivers and lochs.

SS:	1/2000
AV:	F5.0
ISO:	320
FL:	420mm

SS: 1/5000
AV: F5.0
ISO: 400
FL: 420mm

COMMON SANDPIPER

SS: 1/1000
AV: F5.0
ISO: 320
FL: 420mm

168

MAY

OYSTERCATCHER

LOCATION:

THE LOCHS AND LOCHANS OF MULL ———

OYSTERCATCHER

The oystercatcher is easily recognizable with his black head and bright red bill and eye. It has a distinctive peeping call and feeds on shellfish and other crustaceans. The oystercatcher can often be seen trying to break up shellfish on the shore.

SS:	**1/3200**
AV:	**F5.0**
ISO:	**400**
FL:	**420mm**

SS:	**1/320**
AV:	**F5.6**
ISO:	**1000**
FL:	**700mm**

172

MAY

WHEATEAR

LOCATION:

THE LOCHS AND LOCHANS OF MULL

WHEATEAR

Croggan is a particularly reliable place to spot wheatears. The species is widespread in the uplands of the UK during the summer months, and can be found close to most lochs and lochans on Mull. I noticed quite a few wheatears flying about on some rocks not far from this stunning backdrop of yellow gorse bushes. I parked my car close by and waited. It wasn't too long before I was able to capture exactly the shot I was hoping for. If only it was always this straightforward!

SS:	**1/3200**
AV:	**F5.0**
ISO:	**400**
FL:	**420mm**

WHEATEAR

I had just caught a glimpse of this wheatear having a bath in a puddle when he then hopped up to sit on this post to sunbathe for a good five minutes.

SS:	**1/1600**
AV:	**F6.3**
ISO:	**250**
FL:	**700mm**

WHEATEAR

Wheatears arrive in the UK in March to breed, only returning South to Africa in September. They prefer to make their home in open upland habitat, nesting in cavities between rocks. Their diet consists mainly of invertebrates, and I have found that the best way to photograph them is whilst they are looking for food among the rocks, and on the ground nearby.

SS:	1/1000
AV:	F5.6
ISO:	1000
FL:	700mm

FEMALE WHEATEAR

The female wheatear is a blend of brown and orange. They feed on invertebrates and their larvae.

SS: 1/3200
AV: F5.6
ISO: 500
FL: 700mm

MAY

SWALLOW

LOCATION:

CROGGAN

SWALLOW

In summer, just as you reach the shores of Loch Spelve you will likely see swallows being active near an old, ruined wooden building to your right. This bird kept landing on a rusty nail looking up at his nest.

SS:	1/640
AV:	F5.6
ISO:	800
FL:	700mm

182

MAY

RINGED PLOVER

LOCATION:

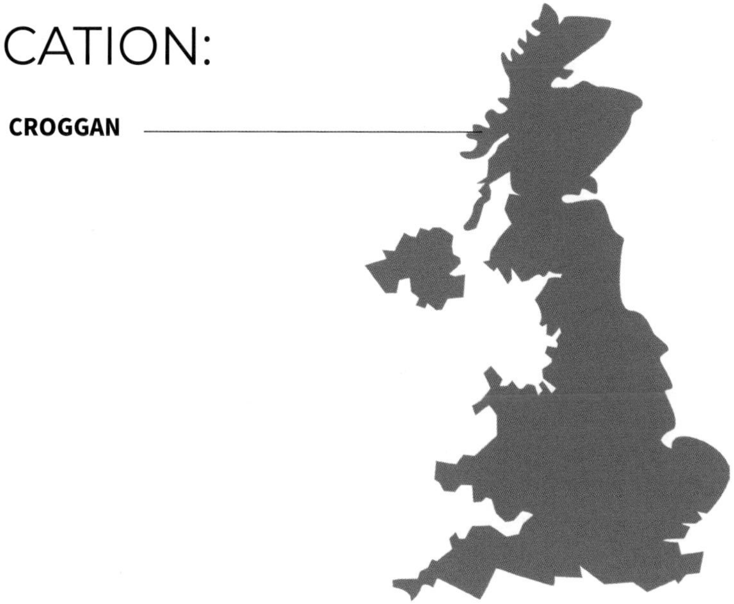

CROGGAN

RINGED PLOVER

I've spotted the ringed plover most years here at Croggan feeding among the rocks and on the grass land looking for worms and other invertebrates. The ringed plover is a small, plump wading bird around 18cm in length. They breed on coastal beaches and are beginning to appear more frequently inland.

SS: 1/800
AV: F7.1
ISO: 1000
FL: 700mm

HOW I TOOK THIS IMAGE

Ringed plovers are tiny little waders and the best way to get a nice image is to get low to the ground so that your lens is at eye-level to the bird. This is good practice when photographing wildlife generally as the resultant images are almost always more striking. Here, I lay on the rocks near the water's edge and waited for the bird to come close to me.

SS: 1/1000
AV: F5.6
ISO: 2500
FL: 490mm

186

MAY

ROCK PIPIT

LOCATION:

LOCH NA KEAL, MULL ——————

ROCK PIPIT

Loch na Keal is a fine place to see rock pipits. They are often on the grass or amongst the rocks looking for worms. The rock pipit is a stocky type of pipit, larger than the likes of the more common meadow pipit. They breed around the coast, feeding on insects, worms, small shellfish, and other crustaceans.

SS:	1/800
AV:	F5.6
ISO:	4000
FL:	700mm

SS: 1/400
AV: F5.6
ISO: 2500
FL: 700mm

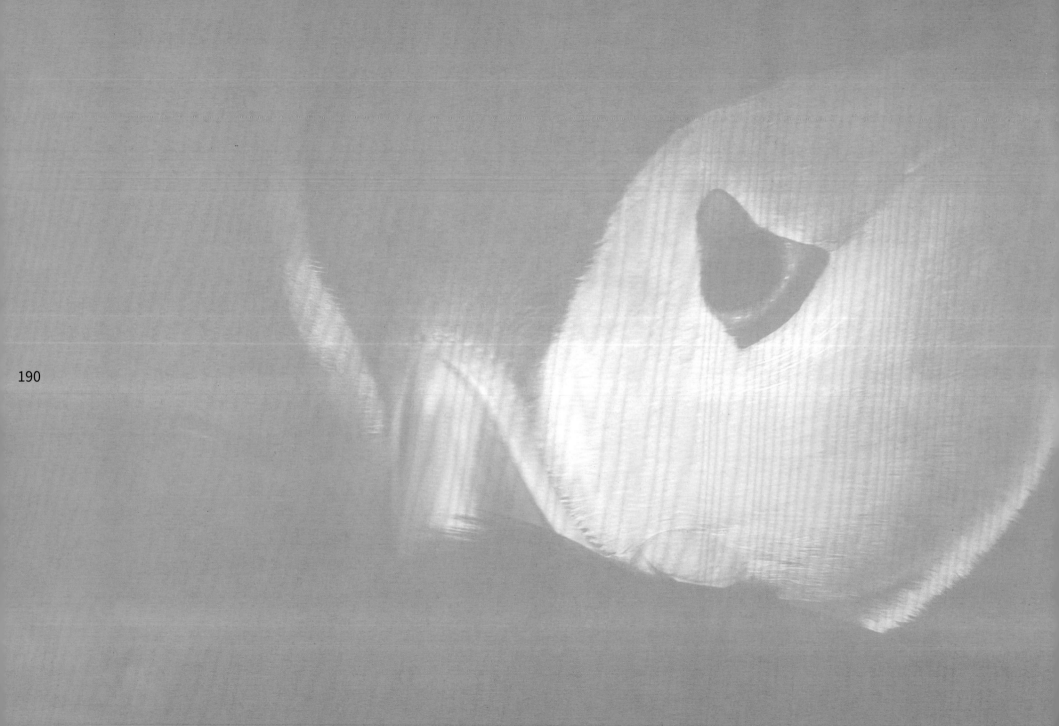

190

MAY

PUFFIN

LOCATION:

LUNGA

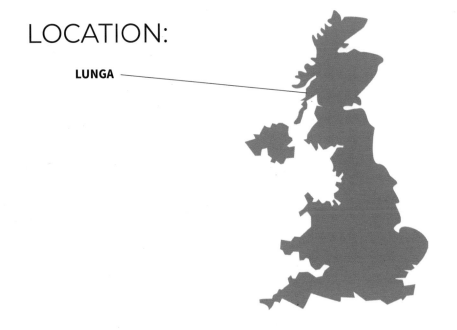

LOCATION: LUNGA

Directions: Ulva Ferry, Turus Mara Boat Tours.

Puffins, which also known as the 'Sea Parrot' are very easily recognized by their distinctive bill. They breed in large colonies on coastal cliffs making their nests in burrows in the soil. They feed on small fish, and sand eels are a firm favourite. The best time to see puffins is from April to late July.

Other places to see puffins:

- Farne Isles, Northumberland
- Bempton Cliffs, Yorkshire
- Isle Of May, Fife
- Skomer Island, Pembrokeshire
- South Stack Cliffs, Anglesey

SS: 1/4000
AV: F4.5
ISO: 400
FL: 180mm

PUFFIN

PUFFIN IN BLUEBELLS

Lunga is a small island just off the coast of Mull. It is probably one of the best places to see puffins in the UK. Being a protected habitat with limited visitor numbers the birds are extremely accessible, with some burrows just few feet away from the trails. May is an excellent time to visit the island because the bluebells are in full bloom and make for an impressive backdrop for your images.

SS:	**1/800**
AV:	**F5.0**
ISO:	**1000**
FL:	**200mm**

SS: 1/4000
AV: F4.5
ISO: 400
FL: 200mm

HIDING

This puffin was hiding away in a little rock crevice. I lay on the ground to photograph him and he tucked his head in his feathers. He certainly appeared to be very shy.

SS: 1/250
AV: F5.6
ISO: 640
FL: 400mm

198

JUNE

CURLEW

LOCATION:

REDMIRE MOOR, GRINTON MOOR, HELWITH MOOR (MARSKE), YORKSHIRE

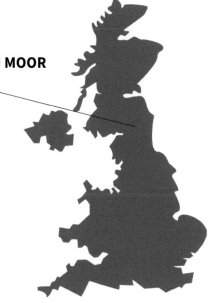

LOCATION: NORTH YORKSHIRE

Location: Redmire Moor, Grinton Moor, Helwith Moor (Marske),
All in North Yorkshire.

Curlews can be seen around coastlines with Morecambe Bay being one of the best places to see them. Large numbers can be seen throughout North Yorkshire on moorlands. The Curlew is a large wader similar in size to a pheasant. It can be seen from February until July on wet grasslands, farmland and heath moorlands. It has a very long, distinctive curved bill and its call is an extremely eerie, repeating trill of 'cur-lee'.

200

Nesting Birds

May and June is a good time to see woodland, upland, and moorlands birds. In fact, most birds raise their broods during these months making it the prime time of year to observe them feeding their young. Please do stay at a distance to avoid any chance of disturbance.

CALL OF THE CURLEW

The curlew is a very wary, and shy bird and will generally fly off the moment it catches a glimpse of you. May and June are particularly good months to capture closer shots as they will stay close to their young. Don't approach too closely - you will cause distress and this might affect the chances of raising the chicks to adulthood.

SS:	1/4000
AV:	F6.3
ISO:	800
FL:	700mm

SS: 1/2500
AV: F5.6
ISO: 640
FL: 700mm

CURLEW IN HEATHER

SS:	1/3200
AV:	F5.6
ISO:	640
FL:	700mm

SS: 1/400
AV: F7.1
ISO: 640
FL: 700mm

AND, HE'S OFF!

This curlew chick looks like he's running for his life! Surely I'm not that scary. I quite liked this image, it's a bit different and very comical - I also loved how the light was falling on the youngster.

SS:	**1/1600**
AV:	**F5.6**
ISO:	**400**
FL:	**700mm**

JUNE
LAPWING

LOCATION:

REDMIRE MOOR, GRINTON MOOR, HELWITH MOOR (MARSKE), YORKSHIRE

LOCATION: NORTH YORKSHIRE

Lapwings can be seen not only in North Yorkshire but also throughout the UK.

These very pretty waders are usually found on wetlands, as well as farmland, heathland and moorlands. They are often seen in sizeable flocks, and individually as they perform their incredible flying 'displays'. They have a distinctive call which lends them their 'Peewit' nickname. They nest on the ground, directly on the grass or soil. It's difficult to mistake the lapwing for any other bird due to its lon crest and striking plumage colouration. Whilst they appear to be black and white at a distance, they are in fact an extremely colourful bird with an iridescent hue and flashes of green and purple across their darker feathers.

SS: 1/250
AV: F5.6
ISO: 100
FL: 700mm

JUVENILE LAPWING

I was watching these young lapwing chicks for some time waiting for them to emerge from the undergrowth. When they eventually came into full view I was able to fire off the shutter whilst the bird was between me and the sun resulting in this lovely backlit image.

SS:	1/2000
AV:	F5.6
ISO:	400
FL:	700mm

JUNE

SNIPE

LOCATION:

REDMIRE MOOR, GRINTON MOOR, HELWITH MOOR (MARSKE), YORKSHIRE

LOCATION: NORTH YORKSHIRE

The snipe is a medium-sized wading bird with a long straight bill. They are widespread throughout the UK and can be found on heath moorland and farmland especially during springtime where you can often find them sitting on fence posts.

216

SS: 1/6400
AV: F5.6
ISO: 2500
FL: 400mm

SNIPE CALLING

This snipe has been captured as it calls out for its young in absolutely glorious light.

SS: 1/800
AV: F5.6
ISO: 800
FL: 700mm

HOW I TOOK THIS IMAGE

Snipes are a very nervous bird and this makes getting close to photograph them rather difficult. Having got to know this area particularly well I was aware that snipe were often present. I parked on the grass verge at the side of the moor and used some camouflage to cover the window of my car. I rested my camera on a beanbag with the only the lens exposed and I waited patiently to capture this beautiful bird in the frame.

SS: 1/250
AV: F5.6
ISO: 1000
FL: 700mm

SNIPE

SS: 1/1000
AV: F5.6
ISO: 200
FL: 700mm

SS: 1/500
AV: F5.6
ISO: 1250
FL: 700mm

A CURIOUS SNIPE

I had been watching this Snipe for about half an hour, rather confused by its behaviour. Eventually I realised it had a clutch of young at the bottom of the post. They chicks were unfortunately hidden in rather long grass so I was unable to get a shot of them.

SS:	1/250
AV:	F5.6
ISO:	1250
FL:	700mm

224

JUNE

MEADOW PIPIT

LOCATION:

REDMIRE MOOR, GRINTON MOOR, HELWITH MOOR (MARSKE), YORKSHIRE

LOCATION: NORTH YORKSHIRE

One of the very many different species of bird found on the Hawes to Ribblehead road in North Yorkshire, meadow pipits are a small bird which are widespread throughout the country. They are regularly taken advantage of by the cuckoo which is particularly keen on using the meadow pipit's nest to lay their own eggs. It's quite remarkable to see an adult pipit raising the enormous cuckoo chick as though it was their own offspring! Meadow pipits feed on insects, including flies, moths, and catterpillars.

MEADOW PIPIT

SS: 1/1000
AV: F5.6
ISO: 400
FL: 700mm

SS: 1/800
AV: F5.6
ISO: 640
FL: 700mm

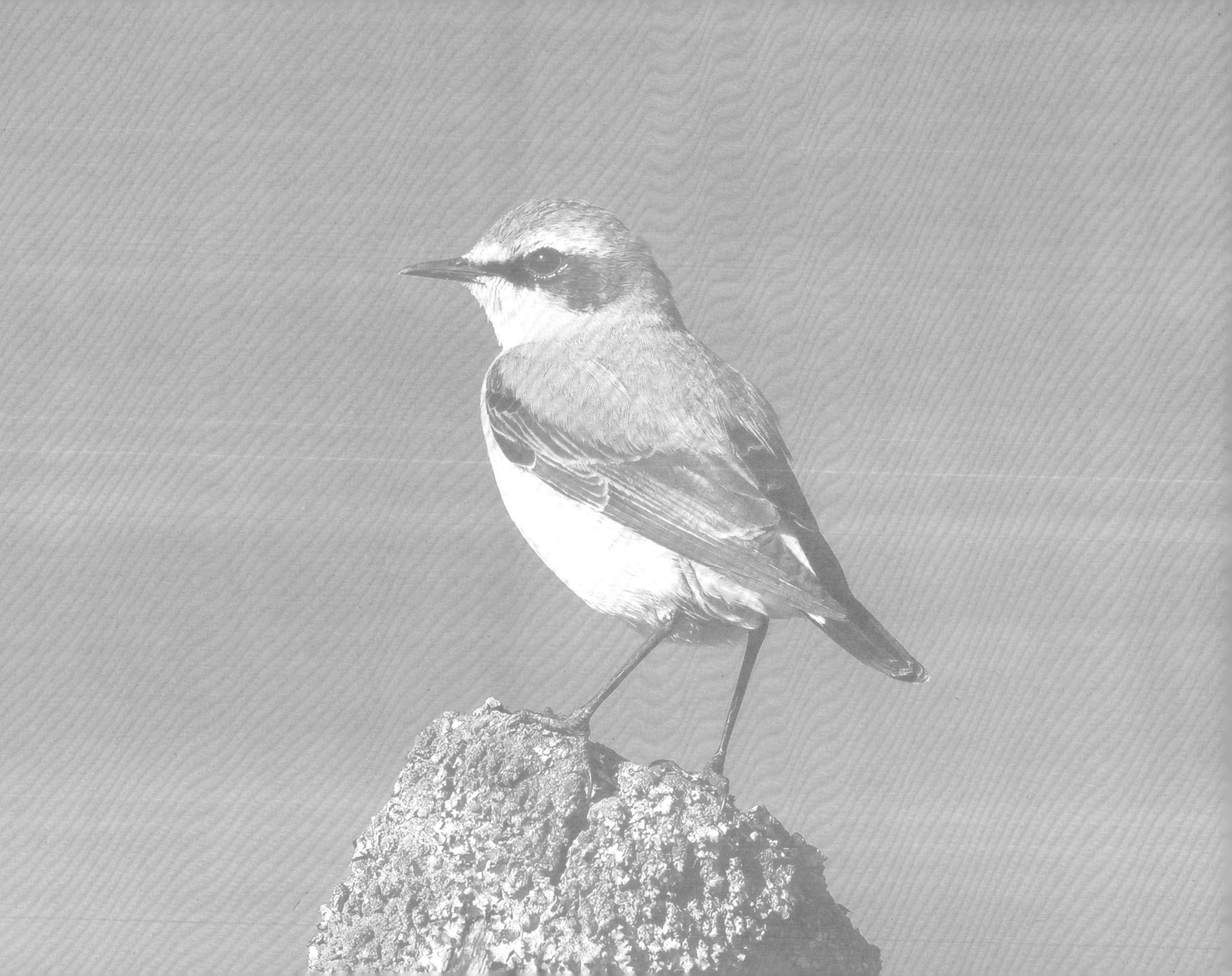

JUNE

WHEATEAR

LOCATION:

REDMIRE MOOR, GRINTON MOOR, HELWITH MOOR (MARSKE), YORKSHIRE

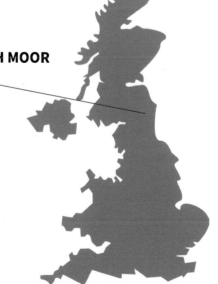

WHEATEAR ON LICHEN CLAD POST

Wheatear are found across the UK and you can read more about them in 'May' when I photographed them on the Isle of Mull.

SS:	1/1250
AV:	F6.3
ISO:	250
FL:	700mm

234

JUNE

SKYLARK

LOCATION:

REDMIRE MOOR, GRINTON MOOR, HELWITH MOOR (MARSKE), YORKSHIRE

LOCATION: NATIONWIDE

Found almost everywhere in the UK, although the birds shown here were seen in North Yorkshire.

The skylark is a small bird which is a touch larger than a house sparrow. It has a distinctive small crest which is often raised when it is alarmed. They feed mainly on insects and can be typically seen on farmland and moorland.

SS: 1/3200
AV: F5.6
ISO: 400
FL: 700mm

SKYLARK

SS: 1/4000
AV: F5.6
ISO: 400
FL: 700mm

239

JUNE

SPOTTED, AND PIED FLYCATCHER

LOCATION:

OSMOTHERLY, NORTH YORKSHIRE

LOCATION: NORTH YORKSHIRE

Take the drive through Osmotherly over the moors and watch out for flycatchers in trees near streams.

Spotted Flycatcher
The spotted flycatcher is a summer visitor which can be seen in open woodlands. They feed on flying insects (particularly butterflies, moths, and craneflies) which they catch in mid-flight.

Pied Flycatcher
The pied flycatcher is also a summer visitor (migrating from Africa to the UK to breed). Whilst they are similar in size and shape to the spotted flycatcher, they have completely different, rather striking, black and white plumage.

SS: 1/160
AV: F5.6
ISO: 2500
FL: 560mm

SPOTTED FLYCATCHER

SS: 1/600
AV: F5.6
ISO: 1250
FL: 500mm

SS: 1/4000
AV: F5.6
ISO: 1000
FL: 700mm

SPOTTED FLYCATCHER

SS: 1/640
AV: F5.6
ISO: 1250
FL: 513mm

SPOTTED FLYCATCHER

SS: 1/200
AV: F5.6
ISO: 1250
FL: 500mm

248

JUNE

REDSTART

LOCATION:

OSMOTHERLY, NORTH YORKSHIRE

LOCATION: NORTH YORKSHIRE

Another bird which can be found in the Osmotherly moors, the redstart is also a summer visitor to the UK. At first glance, it looks similar to a Robin but the male has a red breast and black face and throat. They arrive in the UK during April and can be below the tree-line near streams whilst they search for insect to feed on. They are quite a shy bird, often staying hidden in trees.

250

251

MALE REDSTART

SS: 1/800
AV: F4
ISO: 2000
FL: 500mm

I encouraged this redstart into view by placing mealworms in the hollow of a broken tree stump. I set myself up in a bag hide to camouflage myself, waiting for the bird to appear.

SS: 1/800
AV: F4
ISO: 2000
FL: 500mm

FEMALE REDSTART

This was taken by shooting into a very dark background. This female redstart was feeding her young and was using this perch repeatedly before heading off to find more insects with which to feed her chicks.

JUNE

TREECREEPER

LOCATION:

**CONIFER WOODLAND
THROUGHOUT THE UK**

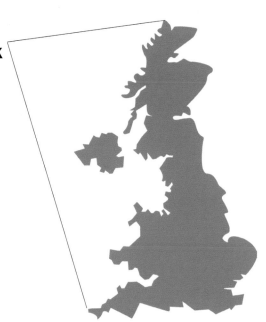

The Treecreeper can be found in both broad-leaf and conifer woodland. They are usually seen creeping up trees looking for food, they feed on insects which they find in the bark of the tree and use their long beaks to pick out their prey. They breed during April and have a clutch of around six eggs.

SS: 1/250
AV: F5.6
ISO: 2500
FL: 560mm

JUVENILE TREECREEPER

SS: 1/250
AV: F5.6
ISO: 640
FL: 349mm

JULY

OSPREY

LOCATION:

AVIEMORE, AND RUTLAND WATER

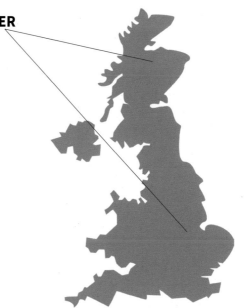

LOCATION: AVIEMORE

Location: Aviemore, and Rutland Water.

The best way to get a really close up photograph of an Osprey grabbing a fish out of the water is to book a hide, there are a few places which offer this now but they don't come cheap. Typical pricing is at around £130 a session (2020)

Aviemore Ospreys
www.aviemoreospreys.co.uk

Rothiemurchus
www.rothiemurchus.net

Horn Mill Osprey Hide (Rutland)
www.rivergwashtroutfarm.co.uk

The osprey is a fish-eating bird of prey which feeds mostly on salmon and trout. Watching an osprey hunt is a memorable experience indeed. For many years I've said it is one of my fondest experiences with nature - watching the bird fly above the water as they scouting for fish. Once the osprey spots a fish it will dive down to grab it from just below the surface with its talons. Quite often the bird will be practically submerged at this point so it can take an incredible amount of effort to get airborne again, especially with a large trout in its grasp. The osprey breeds between April and July with pairs frequently returning to breed with each other year after year. They nest high up in tall trees which are usually close to water. In autumn they return to sub-Saharan Africa.

SS: 1/2000
AV: F2.8
ISO: 2500
FL: 300mm

SS: 1/8000
AV: F2.8
ISO: 400
FL: 300mm

OSPREY IN WATER

SS:	1/8000
AV:	F2.8
ISO:	400
FL:	300mm

OSPREY

Ospreys fly above the water looking for prey, often at heights of up to seventy metres. They plunge down with talons outstretched to catch a fish.

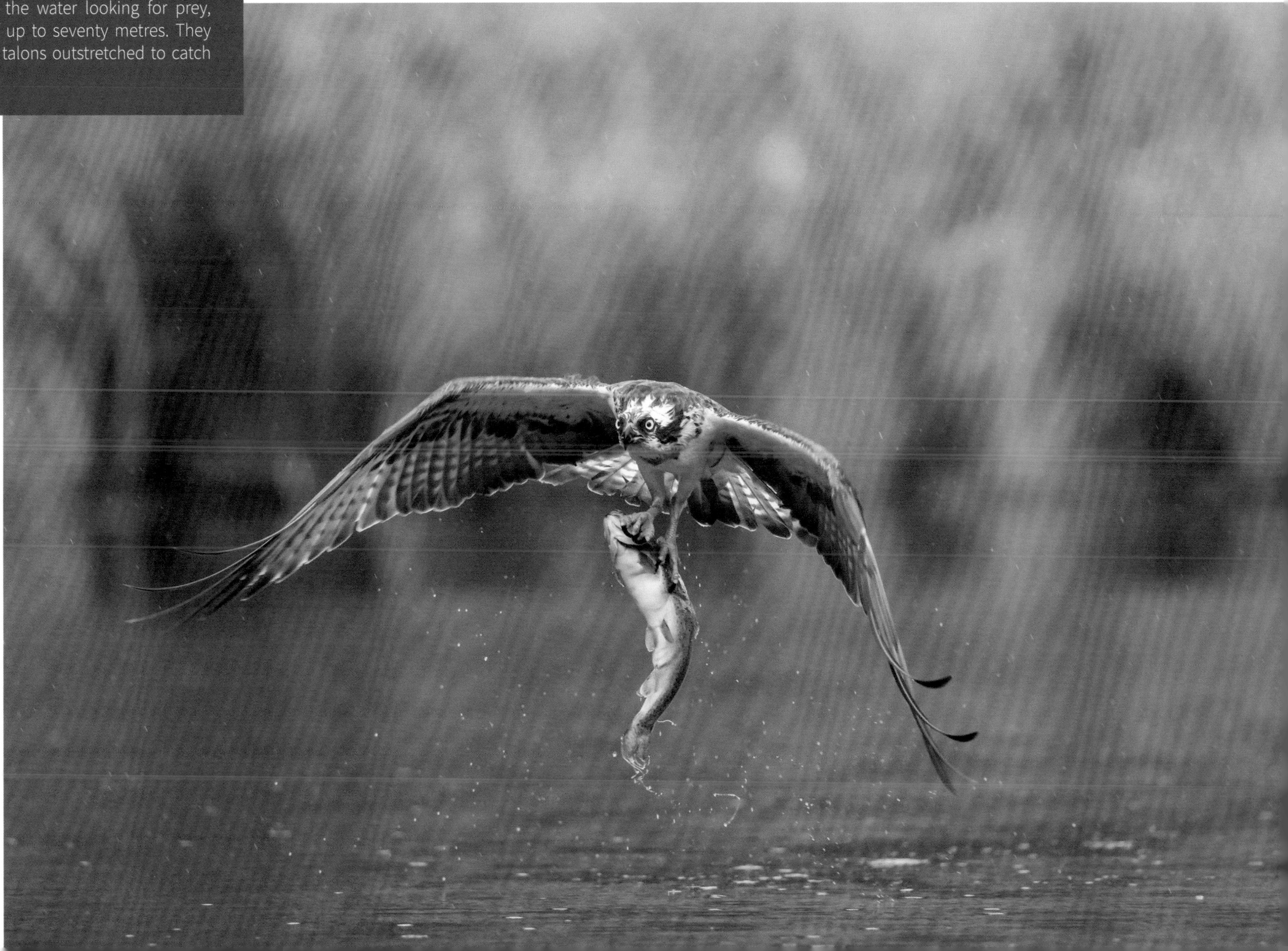

SS:	**1/800**
AV:	**F4.0**
ISO:	**3200**
FL:	**500mm**

OSPREY WITH TROUT

Ospreys build a large nest known as an 'eyrie' at the top of a large tree. They often use the same nest for many years.

SS:	1/4000
AV:	F2.8
ISO:	300
FL:	300mm

JULY

KINGFISHER

LOCATION:

RIVERBANKS THROUGHOUT THE UK

LOCATION: NATIONWIDE

Location: Riverbanks throughout the UK, and in particular:

St Aidens RSPB, Fairburn Ings RSPB

Kingfisher Hide Set Ups

Mark Hughes
https://markhughesimages.net

Tom Robinson
https://www.wildlife-photography-hides.co.uk

Mike Dunlevy
https://www.mikedunlevy.co.uk

Kingfishers can often be seen darting low to the water along riverbanks or sitting quietly on a perch looking for their next meal.

They are a striking small bird of around 17cm in length with a bright blue back and orange breast. Both adults have a black bill and the female kingfisher has an orange patch on the lower part of her bill. They live in burrows or holes in riverbanks. June and July are a good time to see them as they are often very busy feeding their young.

KINGFISHER EATING A FISH

This image was captured at Mark Hughes' kingfisher hide near Leeds. The bird frequently sat on this perch where she dived down for fish. More often than not she would fly of immediately after a successful dive, but on this occasion she stayed on the perch whilst she swalloed the fish whole giving me the opportunity to take this fabulous shot.

SS:	**1/1250**
AV:	**F5.6**
ISO:	**800**
FL:	**448mm**

This bird chose a teasel from which to eye up her next meal.

SS: 1/1250
AV: F5.6
ISO: 800
FL: 470mm

KINGFISHER SITTING ON GOPRO

SS:	**1/2500**
AV:	**F5.6**
ISO:	**800**
FL:	**480mm**

SS: 1/1100
AV: F6.3
ISO: 3200
FL: 142mm

KINGFISHER FLYING OFF WITH A FISH

SS: 1/1100
AV: F6.3
ISO: 3200
FL: 142mm

HOW I TOOK THIS IMAGE

This image was taken by pre-focusing on an area where the Kingfisher was known to dive. I placed a stick below the perch where the kingfisher would had been regularly sitting and used this stick to act as a focal point. I removed the stick, switching the camera onto manual focus to prevent it from automatically refocussing. I selected a high-speed shutter mode and used a remote control to remove the chance of camera-shake. At the precise moment the kingfisher left the perch to dive I fired the shutter knowing that I had the best possible chance of getting a shot in sharp focus. This technique requires quite a few attempts to get just right, and a bit of luck is always welcomed!

SS: 1/3200
AV: F7.1
ISO: 6400
FL: 140mm

KINGFISHER SITTING ON A BRANCH

SS: 1/200
AV: F5.6
ISO: 2000
FL: 350mm

SS: 1/160
AV: F8.0
ISO: 1000
FL: 180mm

284

AUGUST

RED GROUSE

LOCATION:

REDMIRE, NORTH YORKSHIRE

LOCATION: NORTH YORKSHIRE

The red grouse is a medium-sized, rather plump game bird. It is reddish-brown in colour with white feathers on legs. They are found on upland heaths and moors of North Yorkshire, and in similar habitat throughout the UK where they feed on the heather. August is generally the best time to photograph them as the heather is in full bloom.

286

SS: 1/2500
AV: F4
ISO: 800
FL: 400mm

ALL FLUFFED UP

Red grouse feed on the tips of heather. Being a ground-nesting bird, their young are extremely vulnerable to predators. Consequently their brood sizes can be quite large with up to nine or ten chicks in a single clutch.

SS:	**1/2500**
AV:	**F4**
ISO:	**200**
FL:	**400mm**

SS: 1/1600
AV: F4
ISO: 200
FL: 400mm

FEMALE RED GROUSE

HOW I TOOK THIS IMAGE

I lay on the ground so I could get eye level to the grouse and waited for her to pop her head up out of the heather. Thankfully, she looked straight down the lens, rewarding me with this portrait.

SS:	1/4000
AV:	F4.0
ISO:	1000
FL:	500mm

SS: 1/5000
AV: F4.0
ISO: 1600
FL: 500mm

MALE RED GROUSE

On the morning I captured this photograph I was blessed with perfect, soft light. I had spotted this grouse feeding in the heather and was able to get down just low enough and used a shallow depth of field to keep the background out of focus.

SS:	**1/3200**
AV:	**F4.0**
ISO:	**640**
FL:	**500mm**

SS: 1/1200
AV: F5.6
ISO: 640
FL: 560mm

294

AUGUST

DOLPHINS

LOCATION:

CHANONRY POINT, NEAR INVERNESS

LOCATION: CHANONRY POINT

Chanonry Point is possibly one of the best places to see and photograph dolphins in the wild, but be warned, it gets very busy and parking is limited. Whilst the dolphins here can be seen at any time, you can increase your chances by visiting around an hour after low tide. This is when they tend to chase the salmon in, and can often be seen breaching the surface performing incredible aerial acrobatics.

296

SS: 1/4000
AV: F4
ISO: 1250
FL: 300mm

298

SEPTEMBER

KESTREL

LOCATION:

FARMLAND AND GRASSLAND ACROSS THE UK

LOCATION: NATIONWIDE

Location: Farmland and grassland across the UK.

The kestrel is a small bird of prey which can be seen hunting over open habitats like farmland and grassland. It is also quite often seen hovering over grass verges on roads and motorways. Their diet mostly consists of voles and they have fantastic eyesight. It has been established that kestrels are able to detect the ultraviolet light, given off by urine trails made by rodents! Kestrels often nest in holes in trees as well as in old deserted buildings. They lay up to five eggs, which, when hatched, are fed by both parents for about five weeks until they fledge.

HOW I TOOK THIS IMAGE

This image was captured by baiting a perch with a mouse close to where Kestrels had just fledged from their nest inside an old ruined building. After a few days they started coming down a few times a day. I sat in a pop up hide for around twelve hours a day for more than a week before getting these images.

TWO FOR TEA

SS: 1/250
AV: F10
ISO: 800
FL: 400mm

THREE'S A CROWD

This female kestrel was watching over her young as they tussled over a mouse which she had just brought in.

SS:	1/800
AV:	F7.1
ISO:	800
FL:	234mm

Here, the female kestrel stands over a mouse ready for the kill.

SS: 1/640
AV: F7.1
ISO: 500
FL: 330mm

SS: 1/1100
AV: F6.3
ISO: 3200
FL: 142mm

DANGER AHEAD

In this image the two juvenile kestrels are calling out an alarm to warn of a passing buzzard flies past. Their mother was soon on the case to chase the buzzard away.

SS: 1/1000
AV: F7.1
ISO: 800
FL: 321mm

SEPTEMBER

SPARROWHAWK

LOCATION:

WIDESPREAD THROUGHOUT THE UK

LOCATION: NATIONWIDE

Location: Widespread throughout the UK. Heathlands, farmland, woodlands, towns and cities

The sparrowhawk is a small bird of prey and one of Britain's most prolific killers. They can be found throughout the country in all habitats and often frequent gardens looking for prey. They feed mostly on a diet of small birds such as tits and finches. They build their nests in trees using twigs and lay up to five eggs between May and July. The chicks usually fledge around four weeks after hatching.

This male sparrowhawk spread his wings and stood in a defensive stance as a kestrel swooped past.

SS: 1/125
AV: F11
ISO: 2000
FL: 500mm

FEMALE SPARROWHAWK

SS:	1/500
AV:	F4.5
ISO:	1000
FL:	280mm

Male sparrowhawks are arguably more distinctive than the more subtly-plumaged female. He has a reddish-orange breast and a blue-grey back with striking yellow eyes.

SS: 1/640
AV: F6.3
ISO: 1000
FL: 500mm

DINNER TIME

This female sparrowhawk was feeding on a finch which had been placed on a perch at a taken at a hide set-up in Dumfries. I had sat for over eight hours on this occasion and was only half an hour from throwing in the towel when gorgeous female sparrowhawk made an appearance. It is often the case wildlife photography that a day passes without any activity at all, but when it does it can be very rewarding indeed.

SS:	**1/800**
AV:	**F5.6**
ISO:	**1600**
FL:	**400mm**

THE HUNT

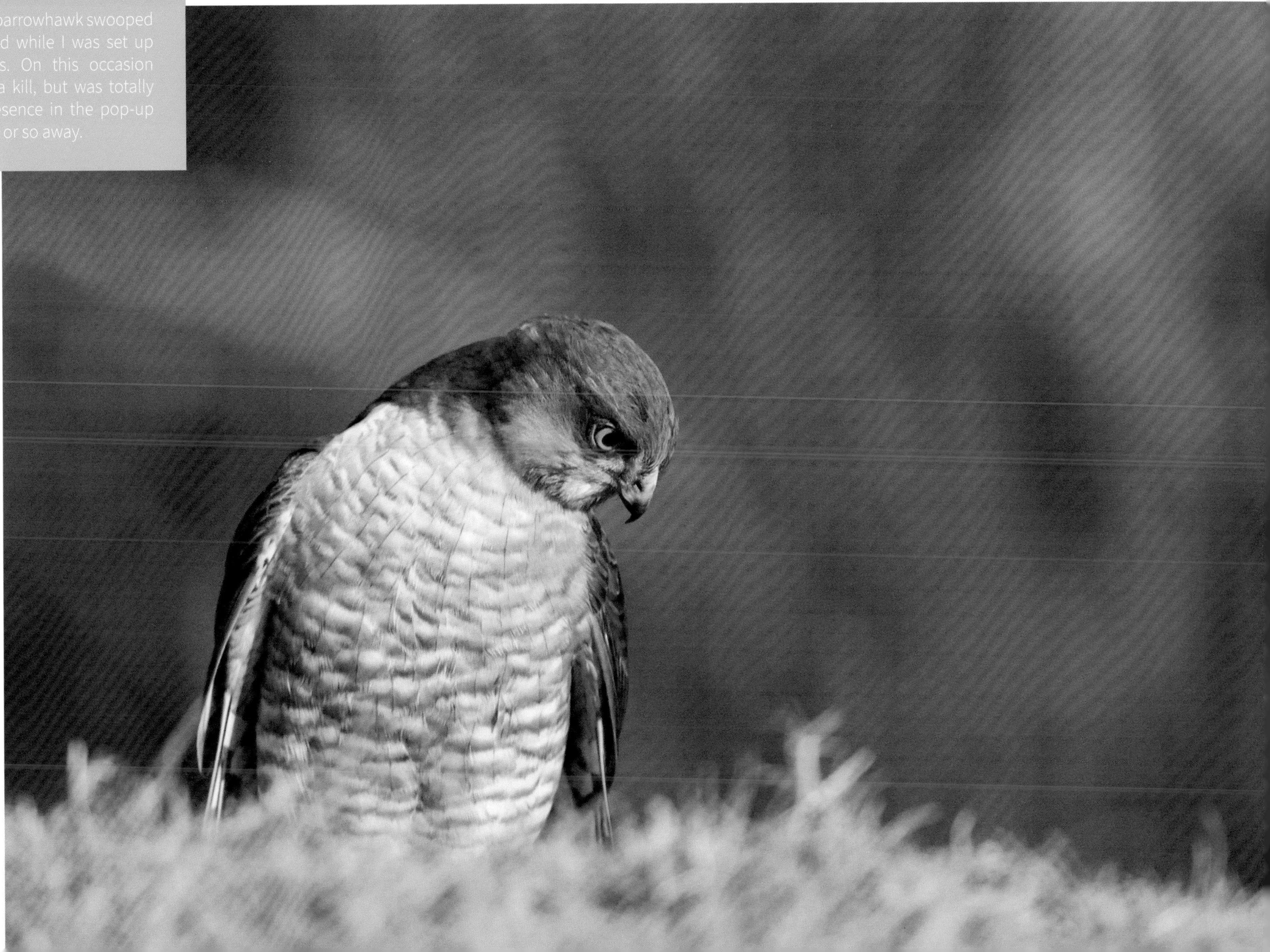

SS: 1/4000
AV: F5.6
ISO: 1250
FL: 560mm

JUVENILE SPARROWHAWK (FEMALE)

Female sparrowhawks can be up to 25% larger than the male. This juvenile had only recently fledged and had made a very poor attempt at catching a chaffinch. In time she would become a highly efficient, and deadly assassin.

SS: 1/1000
AV: F6.3
ISO: 1000
FL: 500mm

These juvenile sparrowhawks are just days from fledging. Their nests are usually built in the canopy of a tree using twigs as can be seen in this image.

SS: 1/80
AV: F11
ISO: 2000
FL: 200mm

SPARROWHAWK WITH KILL

SS: 1/800
AV: F4.0
ISO: 250
FL: 266mm

318

OCTOBER

RED DEER

LOCATION:

SCOTTISH HIGHLANDS

LOCATION: SCOTTISH HIGHLANDS

Location: Glen Etive, Bridge Of Orchy, Highlands.

The best time to photograph red deer stags rutting is during the two hours before and after sunrise and sunset. This is when they are at their most vocal. During the day they tend to head up high in the mountains to graze.

SS: 1/800
AV: F4.0
ISO: 2000
FL: 500mm

THE WARRIOR

SS:	**1/1600**
AV:	**F4.0**
ISO:	**640**
FL:	**500mm**

HOW I CAPTURED 'THE WARRIOR'

'The Warrior' picture is one of my favourites, not least because it was the closest I have ever been to a potentially life-threatening encounter with wildlife. The Warrior was quite happily grazing for well over an hour and was totally at ease with me being around. Despite thinking I had kept a safe distance, he stood upright and fixed a glare which felt as though it could kill me you at twenty paces. Goosebumps ran down my arms and a cold shiver went down my spine - it was utterly chilling. This incredible stag had the look of anger about him - I tried not to make eye contact with him. It wasn't easy because I wanted to be aware of where he was at all times. The Warrior rubbed his antlers in the grass and at that moment, I instinctively fired off a few shots with my camera and he charged...

Time stood still as he raced toward me. I froze, and was almost blown over as he dashed past. I wheeled around only to discover that he had in fact been charging at another stag who was in the process of beating a hasty retreat. The whole thing was something of a blur. Even though The Warrior was not at all bothered with me, the encounter was a stark lesson in the respect that nature deserves. A rutting red deer stag could inflict a deadly blow in the blink of an eye. To this day I will never ever forget the glare he gave me.

CLOSE UP OF STAG BELLOWING

SS: 1/640
AV: F4.0
ISO: 2000
FL: 500mm

YOUNG PRETENDER

This young stag had been getting quite close to another much larger stag over the period of a few days. He looked as though he might be preparing to challenge this older and much bigger opponent but he quickly ran off when the other stag approached. He retreated into a local wood before casting a glance back and then disappeared into the woodland. It would be interesting to know if this young pretender is still around.

SS: 1/200
AV: F4.5
ISO: 2000
FL: 500mm

STAG BELLOWING IN AUTUMN COLOURS

SS: 1/800
AV: F4.0
ISO: 2000
FL: 500mm

NOVEMBER

PINE MARTEN

LOCATION:

CAIRNGORMS, BRIDGE OF CALLY

LOCATION: CAIRNGORMS, BRIDGE OF CALLY

Pine Marten Photography Hides:

Mark Johnson, Penny Hedge (FaceBook), James Roddie

The Pine Marten is mostly found in the North of England and also in the Highlands of Scotland. They are nocturnal which makes them particularly difficult to photograph. Over the past few years wildlife photographers have begun baiting known pine marten territories to give photographers a good chance photographing them from a well-positioned commercial photography hide as the martens come in to feed. The pine marten prefers to live in a woodland habitat and has a wide-ranging diet from rodent and bird's eggs, to fruit and vegetation.

PINE MARTEN

This image was taken late in the evening using a flash set-up. The pine marten here was bailed with nuts and grapes.

SS: 1/160
AV: F7.1
ISO: 800
FL: 360mm

PINE MARTEN

SS: 1/160
AV: F7.1
ISO: 800
FL: 100mm

PINE MARTEN

This image shows a pine marten climbing up a branch looking for food.

SS: 1/160
AV: F7.1
ISO: 800
FL: 107mm

PINE MARTEN KIT

This pine marten kit was standing on some rocks scouting the area. The picture was taken around an hour before sunset.

SS:	1/1250
AV:	F2.8
ISO:	1600
FL:	300mm

SS: 1/2000
AV: F2.8
ISO: 1600
FL: 300mm

PINE MARTEN KIT

Pine martens usually have up to five kits in a litter which are in March or April. The kits usually venture outside at about six weeks old.

SS:	**1/1250**
AV:	**F5**
ISO:	**1250**
FL:	**220mm**

TWO PINE MARTEN KITS

These two pine marten kits are licking their lips as they look for food. In summer it is reported that 30% of their diet consists of bilberries.

SS: 1/400
AV: F4
ISO: 1250
FL: 200mm

Pine martens may look cute and cuddly but they are in fact one of the most fearsome predators in the UK. They have even been known to kill grey squirrels but thankfully they do not appear to be able to catch the more nimble reds. It is quite often the case that pine martens inhabit the same woodland territories as red squirrel.

SS: 1/640
AV: F5
ISO: 1250
FL: 200mm

PINE MARTEN

SS: 1/2500
AV: F5.6
ISO: 1000
FL: 361mm

342

DECEMBER

BARN OWL

LOCATION:

WIDESPREAD THROUGHOUT THE UK

LOCATION: WIDESPREAD

Barn owls are widespread throughout the UK. These images were captured from Leyburn to Hawes, and from Hardraw to Carperby in the Yorkshire Dales

I have regularly seen as many as eight barn owls on these two stretches of road. Watch out for them at dawn and dusk hunting across farmland.

Another location which is excellent for watching and photographing barn owls is the Westerdale to Yorkshire Cycle Hub, YO21 2AP. There are usually many pairs of owls to be seen. They tend to emrge to hunt daily just before the entrance to the Cycle Hub itself which conveniently offers excellent home cooked meals.

Barn Owls are often seen flying low over open countryside as they hunt for mice and voles. Farmland and roadside verges are particularly good habitats to watch barn owls. Sadly though, many barn owls are lost each year to a different type of predator - the motor car. The birds nest in barns or cavities of trees any time from April to August and can even raise a second brood if the food source is plentiful. Wintertime is a particularly good time to photograph these owls due to first light being at a more manageable time of the day. It's often the case that barn owls will be more active after a few days of bad weather. They tend to avoid hunting when they are likely to get wet, waiting for the next dry spell to make a foray for food.

BARN OWL

HOW I TOOK THIS IMAGE

I took this image from a pop-up hide in an area where barn owls had been hunting regularly. I noticed that this bird had begun to land on posts in the field so I set up my hide and waited. Within thirty minutes the owl had landed on the post and I was able to fire off this very close up shot. I wish it was always this easy! The image was more or less full frame with very little crop. Its not often you can get this close to a barn owl in the wild but by using careful fieldcraft and making use of a hide it is possible to get very close to nature indeed.

SS:	1/640
AV:	F5.6
ISO:	1250
FL:	560mm

HOW I TOOK THIS IMAGE

This barn owl had been hunting over farmland for a good week or so and I noticed he had started landing on a freshly cut hedgerow. I decided to park my car on the grass verge on the opposite side of the road and waited. I watched him hunting for an hour and although he landed on the hedgerow he was just too far away to get a good capture. I persevered over the next few days and was eventually presented with the opportunity to take this image in glorious light from the sunrise - just what I was hoping for!

SS: 1/250
AV: F5.6
ISO: 1250
FL: 400mm

BARN OWL

SS: 1/5000
AV: F5.6
ISO: 1250
FL: 500mm

This bird had been quartering the farmland at the same time every morning over the poeriod of a few days. I parked on the on the grass verge using my car as a hide and waited for him to appear. He sat on a fence post about 10 metres from me. Barn owls tend not to pay too much attention to cars which makes them the perfect phtography hide. I do tend to camouflage material over teh window aperture so that they birds are not able to see the human shape through the window.

SS: 1/3200
AV: F5.6
ISO: 1250
FL: 540mm

BARN OWL ON BROKEN FENCE

This owl was sitting patiently on a fence watching for prey. Once again, I had used my car as a hide.

SS:	1/640
AV:	F5.6
ISO:	1250
FL:	560mm

HOW I TOOK THIS IMAGE

After half and hour or so observing this owl as it hunted, I noticed that it was regularly pausing on fence posts in a farmer's field. This particular post was very close to a barn whose doors were left open. I was able to crawl into a position where I could shoot straight into the open doors putting the owl directly in front of a completely dark background. The resulting images looked very much like it had been taken with a flash set-up.

SS: **1/500**
AV: **F7.1**
ISO: **2000**
FL: **700mm**

DECEMBER

SHORT-EARED OWL

LOCATION:

WIDESPREAD OVER MOORLAND AND SALT-MARSHES

Location: Widespread over moorlands and salt-marshes

Hawes to Dent, North Yorkshire
Watch for them hunting on either side of main road

Marske Moor, Richmond
Short-eared Owls breed in this area most years.

North Gare, Seaton Carew, Hartlepool
This is a very reliable place to see short-eared owls

Bempton Cliffs RSPB

Unlike the tawny and barn owl, the short-eared owl hunts during the daytime. The best place to find them is over moorland hunting for mice and voles. They nest on the ground in scraped out hollows and their breeding success is entirely dependent on how good the food source is. They tend to just raise a single brood with the young leaving the nest at quite an early stage.

Short-eared owls are unfazed by the presence of humans will often fly very close-by giving you greater opportunity to capture images whilst they are in-flight. Be aware though that short-eared owls can fly very fast whiles they are hunting, quite unlike the barn owl.

SS: 1/1600
AV: F6.3
ISO: 640
FL: 700mm

SHORT-EARED OWL

SS: 1/1250
AV: F6.3
ISO: 640
FL: 700mm

SS: 1/1600
AV: F6.3
ISO: 640
FL: 700mm

SHORT-EARED OWL

This short-eared owl was hovering above grassland on the lookout for voles.

SS:	**1/4000**
AV:	**F4.0**
ISO:	**1000**
FL:	**400mm**

It is truly a great experience simply sitting and watching the short-eared owl hunt with those enormous, piercing yellow eyes.

SS: 1/1250
AV: F6.3
ISO: 640
FL: 700mm

360

DECEMBER

TAWNY OWL

LOCATION:

WIDESPREAD THROUGH BRITAIN IN WOODLAND

LOCATION: WIDESPREAD

Tawny Owls are mainly nocturnal, and they will only tend to venture out in daylight if they are feeding young. Their diet is predominantly made up of mice and voles. Tawny owls are a silent hunter with incredibly sensitive sight and hearing. This means that their prey have very little chance of hearing them descend upon them. Tawnies usually mate for life, laying their eggs in cavities in trees. It is much more likely that you will hear a tawny owl than actually seeing one. Their distinctive 'hoo-hoo hoo-hoo' call is made by the male, and the female makes the higher-pitched 'kew-wick' sound.

SS: 1/160
AV: F13
ISO: 1000
FL: 200mm

SLEEPING TAWNY

This tawny owl had been going to roost in the same barn as some of the little owls which I had been observing. The barn is split into three separate rooms and I am fortunate to be able to watch two species of owl in the same barn. The tawny had started sitting in the window offering an excellent composition with the weather-beaten frame, the broken panes full of cobwebs and the weeds growing in front of the opening.

SS:	**1/640**
AV:	**F4.0**
ISO:	**400**
FL:	**400mm**

The tawny owl had been gradually encouraged to visit a post using bait and after a while it became comfortable coming down to feed. I used a two speedlights and set them so that they were just bright enough to 'freeze' the bird in flight.

SS:	**1/160**
AV:	**F13**
ISO:	**1000**
FL:	**200mm**

TAWNY OWL

SS: 1/160
AV: F13
ISO: 1000
FL: 200mm

SS: 1/160
AV: F13
ISO: 1000
FL: 200mm

DECEMBER

LITTLE OWL

LOCATION:

**MOST COMMON IN
THE SOUTHERN HALF OF THE UK**

LOCATION: NORTH YORKSHIRE

Little Owls can be seen around England and parts of Wales on farmlands and open woodland.

Some of the more reliable spots to find little owls:

Leyburn to Wensley Road
This stretch is around a mile long - watch out for a single owl sitting on top of a barn on the left hand side. At the Three Horseshoes pub turn right for Redmire. About 2 miles on left hand side keep an eye out on barns, we have a breeding pair along here which you should see especially if you go between 7pm and 9pm.

Aysgarth to Hawes Road
Watch out for birds on posts and barns along this stretch.

As the name suggests, little owls are very small. They stand around 20cm making them the smallest owl in the UK. Their diet consists of small mammals such as mice and voles, and they also feed on invertebrates. Hunting tends to take place at dawn and dusk and these birds usually pair up for life, making their nest in small holes in trees or on a platform in a disused building. Their young typically hatch between May and July.

HOW I TOOK THIS IMAGE

LITTLE OWL

There are a few barns in the Yorkshire Dales where I have located little owls and they can be spotted in them quite regularly. On this occasion I did not want to just photograph the bird sitting on a ledge with the barn face-on. I wanted to capture the owl peeping around the corner of the building with a nice clutter-free background. Once I had established that the owl was present, I drove past the barn to park my car. I then crept up very quietly indeed to get level with the edge of the barn and he sat looking at me as if he knew I was coming. Realising that I was on borrowed time, I quickly fired off my shot before he flew off. Little owls are extremely wary so its always not easy to get close to them. It is often that case that either fieldcraft or a hide is required.

SS: 1/640
AV: F5.6
ISO: 1250
FL: 560mm

LITTLE OWL

HOW I TOOK THIS IMAGE

This is another image of a little owl on a different barn (near Worton). On this occasion I decided to shoot straight at the owl. Both of these images are very nice, but I have a preference for the image where the owl is peering round the edge of the barn.

SS:	1/5000
AV:	F2.8
ISO:	800
FL:	300mm

SS: 1/2000
AV: F5.6
ISO: 800
FL: 560mm

LITTLE OWL

This image was taken from a little owl hide set-up which took me more than half a year to get them coming in to view. I spent a lot of time doing fieldcraft and discovered that two little owls were roosting in a stone barn in the Yorkshire Dales. I contacted the farmer who was kind enough to let me set up some posts and perches in view of a two-berth pop-up hide. I placed some plastic containers on the back of the posts and filled with mealworms twice a day. Eventually I gained the trust of these very nervous owls and they began to feed here daily after around six months. This photograph came after I had been in the hide for almost five hours at minus six degrees celsius. As with most owls, little owls do not like bad weather so I watched them popping there heads out of the barn window without ever seeming like they were going to come out. Eventually, one of the birds ventured out to feed and I was able to capture this atmospheric shot.

SS:	1/2500
AV:	F4
ISO:	1250
FL:	400mm

SS: 1/2500
AV: F4
ISO: 1250
FL: 400mm

LITTLE OWL

This image shows an adult little owl (left) with juvenile. This was taken from a hide set-up where I had been baiting the post using mealworms.

SS:	**1/2000**
AV:	**F4.0**
ISO:	**800**
FL:	**500mm**

This gorgeous little owlet decided to sit nicely on a post for me after around fourteen hours of following the little guy about.

SS:	1/1250
AV:	F4.0
ISO:	800
FL:	500mm

LITTLE OWL

I saw this owl on one of my more reliable stretches of road. It was sitting on a public footpath sign, but I missed the shot, and he flew into a nearby tree. Not what I was after, but it made a nice composition nonetheless.

SS:	**1/1600**
AV:	**F5.6**
ISO:	**2000**
FL:	**560mm**

LITTLE OWLET

What a lovely little ball of fluff! I found this bird resting in a tree. He is right on the verge of fending for himself and I had only seen his mother once in the four hours I spent watching him.

SS: 1/1000
AV: F4.0
ISO: 800
FL: 500mm

LITTLE OWL

Here is a little owl sitting in a hollow of a tree. She raised two healthy owlets. Unfortunately, the following season jackdaws took over the nest and the little owls were forced to move on.

SS:	**1/125**
AV:	**F4.0**
ISO:	**500**
FL:	**500mm**

OWLET

This image shows an owlet with a mouse which I think was one of the first kills since the bird left its nest.

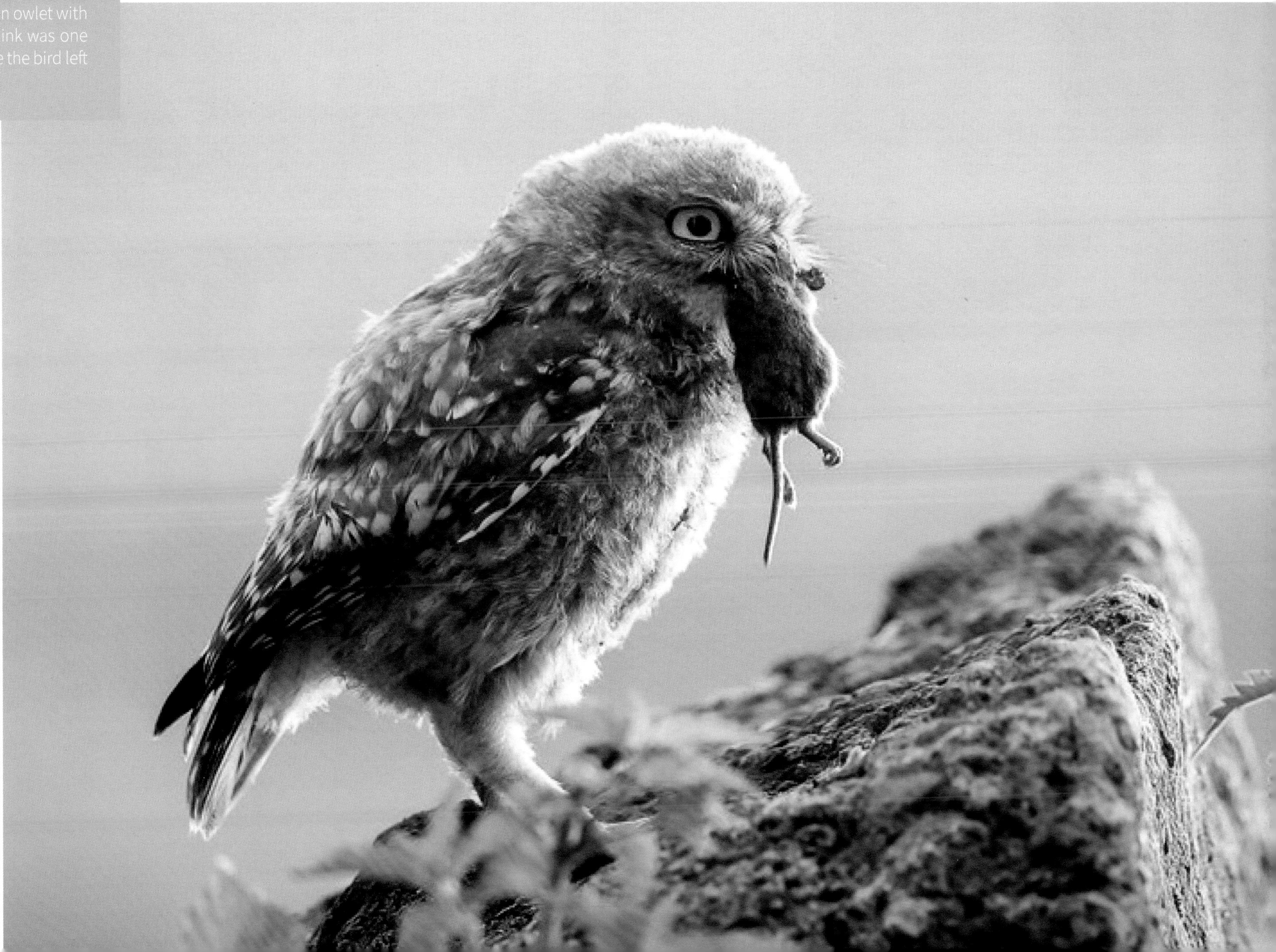

SS: **1/400**
AV: **F4.0**
ISO: **400**
FL: **500mm**

LITTLE OWL

HOW I TOOK THIS IMAGE

This shot, together with the shot on the next page, were taken at my little owl hides. The perches have small plastic food containers screwed into them and I fill them with live mealworms. I am able to use a continuous light which is set at a low power to illuminate the perch and set up two Godox AD200 flashes (one at 1/128 and the other at 1/64 power). It is important to bear in mind that the owls are not in the slightest bit bothered by the flashes. It should never be necessary to put any wildlife in danger for the sake of a photograph.

SS:	1/160
AV:	F5.6
ISO:	500
FL:	560mm

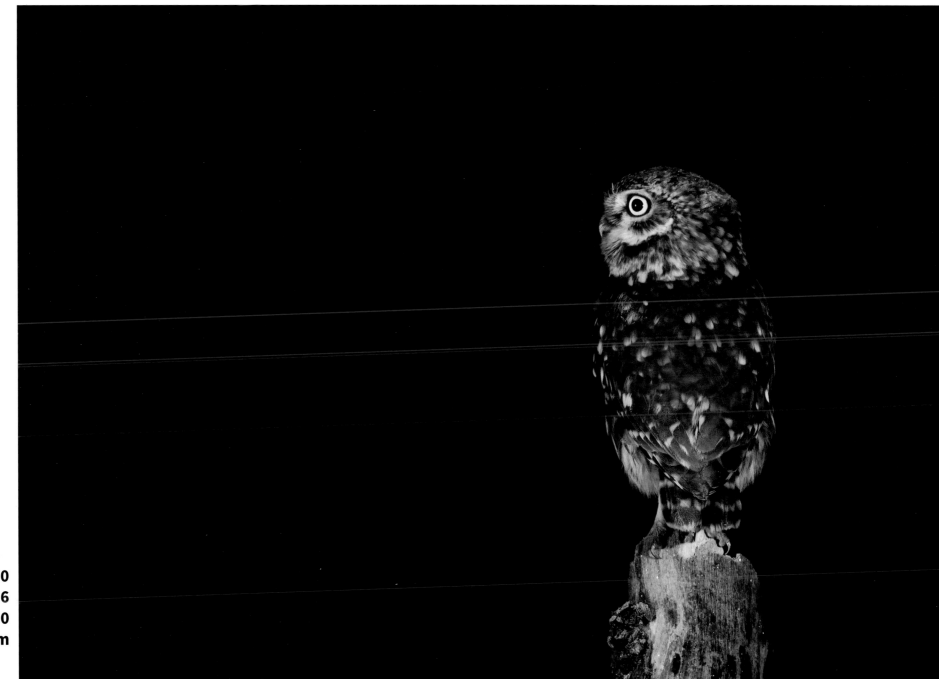

SS: 1/160
AV: F5.6
ISO: 500
FL: 560mm

IN COMING

The little owls were busy feeding their young on the day I got this shot. They were constantly flying back and forth from the nest to a perch which I had baited with a small plastic container of live mealworms. I focused on the perch and locked the lens to manual focus moving it across to eh left just a touch to offset the post from the centre. When the owl flew in I took a burst of shots which resulted in this dynamic image.

SS: 1/4000
AV: F4.0
ISO: 400
FL: 400mm

THREE LITTLE OWLS

This image shows two little owlets standing on a footpath sign and closely watched by their mother. The owlets had fledged at about four weeks and were very quickly growing up.

SS: 1/1000
AV: F7.1
ISO: 1250
FL: 448mm

SS: 1/2000
AV: F4.0
ISO: 2500
FL: 400mm

ON THE TRAILER

In this monochrome shot, this little owl is sitting on a trailer on farmland. He seemed to like sitting at the same spot and often played with the string which you can see hanging down from the trailer.

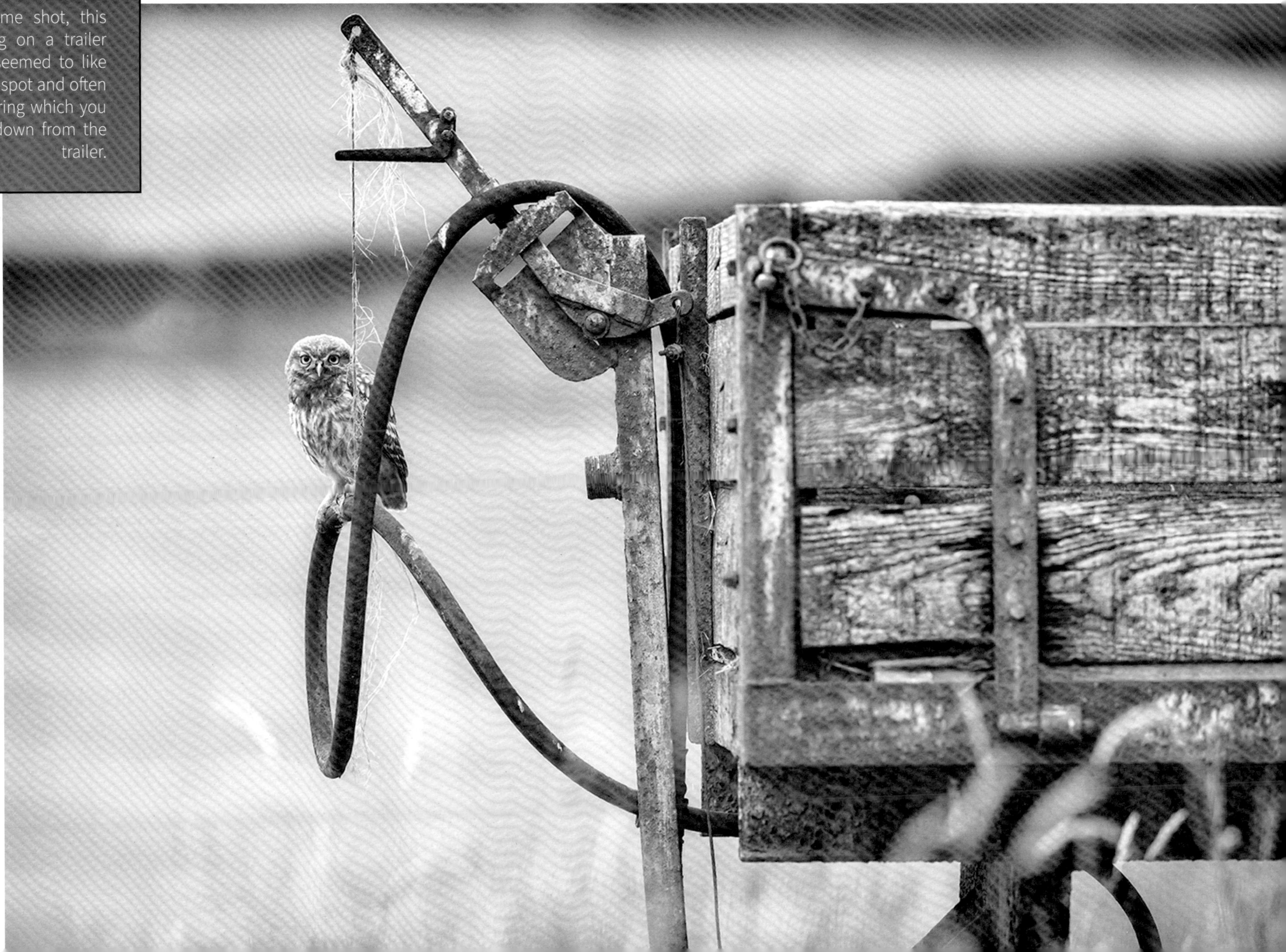

SS: 1/640
AV: F5.6
ISO: 1250
FL: 400mm

PAUL FOWLIE
PHOTOGRAPHY HIDES AND WORKSHOPS

Paul has spent many years locating, observing, and nurturing the perfect environments for photographing species including red deer, dipper, osprey, and red squirrel. In addition, he has established a reputation for leading photography workshops in remote settings across Europe and Scandinavia where he creates unique opportunities for his clients to photograph creatures such as the brown bear, wolverine, and capercaillie.

HIDES

Of all of the hides Paul has carefully positioned, perhaps his most sought after are the woodland hides which, at the time of print, are the only ones of their kind which are available to hire in the UK where it is possible to observe and photograph the remarkable red squirrel.

Paul's hides also offer opportunities to capture images of badgers, roe deer, great spotted woodpecker, together with a whole host of woodland fauna. Having respectfully set up environments after monitoring carefully selected locations over many months, Paul is able to offer once-in-a-lifetime photography opportunities to his clients. The arrangement of his natural apparatus are perfectly positioned to encourage species to approach the photographer in unique and creative ways to offer the potential for images of red squirrels leaping from one platform to another or perhaps a nuthatch or siskin perfectly positioned above a its own, crystal-clear reflection in a pool of water. These incredible locations offer astonishing moments with nature which cannot be found anywhere else.

WORKSHOPS

To complement his hide-based photography settings, Paul also offers a suite of meticulously created wildlife photography workshops in the British countryside and in Europe and Scandinavia. These workshops are well-suited for beginners and experienced wildlife photographers looking to expand their knowledge and skill-set to include new and exciting species and locations.

For more information, and to book a place at one of Paul's hides, or perhaps a spot on his workshops, please visit:

www.paulfowliephotography.co.uk